Also by Karl Giberson

God Saw That It Was Good: A Creation Story for the 21st Century

The Anointed: Evangelical Truth in a Secular Age (with Randall Stephens)

Quantum Leap: How John Polkinghorne Found God in Science and Religion (with Dean Nelson)

The Language of Science and Faith: Straight Answers to Genuine Questions (with Francis Collins)

Saving Darwin: How to Be a Christian and Believe in Evolution

Oracles of Science: Celebrity Scientists versus God and Religion (with Mariano Artigas)

Species of Origins: America's Search for a Creation Story (with Donald Yerxa)

Worlds Apart: The Unholy War Between Religion and Science

THE WONDER OF THE UNIVERSE

Hints of God in Our Fine-Tuned World

KARL W. GIBERSON

IVP Books

An imprint of InterVarsity Press
Downers Grove, Illinois

InterVarsity Press
P.O. Box 1400, Downers Grove, IL 60515-1426
World Wide Web: www.ivpress.com
E-mail: email@ivpress.com

InterVarsity Press® is the book-publishing division of InterVarsity Christian Fellowship/USA®, a movement of students and faculty active on campus at hundreds of universities, colleges and schools of nursing in the United States of America, and a member movement of the International Fellowship of Evangelical Students. For information about local and regional activities, write Public Relations Dept., InterVarsity Christian Fellowship/USA, 6400 Schroeder Rd., P.O. Box 7895, Madison, WI 53707-7895, or visit the IVCF website at <www.intervarsity.org>.

Unless otherwise indicated, all Scripture quotations are taken from the Holy Bible, New Living Translation, *copyright ©1996, 2004. Used by permission of Tyndale House Publishers, Inc., Wheaton, Illinois 60189. All rights reserved.*

Design: Cindy Kiple
Images: Digital Vision/Getty Images

ISBN 978-0-8308-3819-6

Printed in the United States of America ∞

Library of Congress Cataloging-in-Publication Data

Giberson, Karl.
  The wonder of the universe: hints of God in our fine-tuned world/
Karl Giberson.
    p. cm.
  Includes bibliographical references (p.   ) and index.
  ISBN 978-0-8303-3819-6 (pbk.: alk. paper)
  1. Religion and science. I. Title.
  BL240.3.G54 2012
  261.5'5—dc23

2011051593

P	19	18	17	16	15	15	14	13	12	11	10	9	8	7	6	5	4	3	2	1
Y	29	28	27	26	25	24	23	22	21	20	19	18	17	16	15	14	13	12

CONTENTS

INTRODUCTION

Following the Evidence Where It Leads

Only fools say in their hearts, "There is no God."

PSALM 14:1

In 1748 John Wesley founded Kingswood School in Bath, England, a city established as a spa resort by the Romans in A.D. 43 to take advantage of the country's only hot spring. A hero of the Christian faith, Wesley graduated from Oxford University—then a thoroughly Christian institution—and was one of the best-educated scholars of his generation, as well as England's most important religious leader. He believed strongly in education and promoted it consistently throughout his long and productive ministry, which saw him constantly on horseback traveling from village to village. The many preachers he trained were expected to take learning seriously, even as they preached a message of holiness and piety. Wesley established Kingswood to train the sons of his Methodist leaders, whose paltry salaries often made them unable to afford the existing schools, with their well-heeled students. Some years later, in 1894, a companion school to train preachers' daughters, appropriately—at least for the time!—named Queenswood, was established. Kingswood became coeducational in 1978, a development that would surely have alarmed its founder.

Like many of England's long-established schools, Kingswood celebrates distinguished alumni who went on to become leaders in science, politics, business and other fields. Kingswood's leading intellectual alumnus is Antony Flew, one of the most important philosophers of the last half of the twentieth century and, by most measures, his generation's most notorious atheist.

Flew the hard-boiled atheist was nowhere in sight, however, when young Antony enrolled in Wesley's venerable school for the children of ministers, who would have been taken to the woodshed for even flirting with atheism. "I entered Kingswood as a committed and conscientious, if unenthusiastic, Christian," he recalled near the end of his long life.[1] Kingswood, or "KS" as the students called it, promotes itself as a "happy, vibrant and forward-looking school which provides the very best in all round education for pupils aged 3 to 18 years." KS enshrines Wesley's original Christian principles and "all pupils are encouraged to discover a real enthusiasm for learning and a spirit of enquiry."[2]

Figure 0.1. The main building of Kingswood School, founded by John Wesley in 1748 to train the sons of Methodist ministers. One of these sons, Antony Flew, attended in the 1930s as a Christian but went on to become one of the century's leading atheists before embracing deism in his eighties. Flew's late "conversion" to belief in God was very controversial.

Flew reveled in the "spirit of enquiry" at KS—decades before girls were admitted, of course—and with "unrestrained eagerness" he "consumed books on politics, history, science, or almost any topic." Except religion.

He had no real interest in learning about religion and found its various practices to be a "weary duty." Not surprisingly, by the time he finished KS, his childhood faith, shaky and tenuous at best, had disappeared entirely.[3]

THE NOTORIOUS ATHEIST

*We want to stand upon our own feet and look fair and square at the world—
its good facts, its bad facts, its beauties, and its ugliness; see the world as it
is and be not afraid of it. Conquer the world by intelligence and not
merely by being slavishly subdued by the terror that comes from it.*

Bertrand Russell

FLEW WENT ON TO A distinguished career at an almost completely secularized Oxford, rapidly emerging as one of England's leading voices for atheism, debating prominent Christians in Europe and North America. He honed his debating skills at Oxford's venerable Socratic Club, where C. S. Lewis famously defended Christianity and developed apologetic arguments that would appear in books like *Mere Christianity, Miracles* and *The Problem of Pain*. Flew spoke on highbrow BBC radio programs, published in prestigious journals and wrote regularly for the popular media. Wherever arguments supporting belief in God appeared, Flew was there, logical rapier in hand, to demolish them with counterarguments. Or so he thought.

Flew's atheism, solidified by the time he was a wise old man of fifteen, rested on the traditional problem of evil. This has been a perennial problem for belief in God, ever since poor Old Testament Job wondered why his circumstances were going downhill so fast for no apparent reason. If God is good and powerful, why do terrible things, like the 2011 earthquake and tsunami in Japan, happen? Shouldn't a good God want to prevent that? And shouldn't an all-powerful God be capable of doing so? Christian philosophers have puzzled with dismay over this problem of evil for centuries and never resolved it. Anti-Christian philosophers have delighted in it. So Flew, following a path worn smooth by agnostics and atheists before him, rejected God as illogical and contradictory at about the time he was awakening to philosophy. Years later he reflected on this with the theologian Gary Habermas:

> I suppose that the moment when, as a schoolboy of fifteen years, it first appeared to me that the thesis that the universe was created and is sustained by a Being of infinite power and goodness is flatly incompatible

with the occurrence of massive undeniable and undenied evils in that universe, was the first step towards my future career as a philosopher![4]

Decades later, after penning hundreds of pages of arguments against the existence of God, Flew began to have second thoughts.

At the Socratic Club, where Oxford's famous debaters-in-training honed their skills, everyone accepted a rule for thinking that went back more than two thousand years to Plato, where Socrates instructed his students to follow the argument "wherever it leads." This sounds obvious, like fortune-cookie common sense. But it is difficult in practice because we are all humans. Often, as we try to understand the world around us, the evidence leads us in a direction we don't want to go. Perhaps the evidence suggests that our spouse is cheating on us or that our singing voice is terrible or that our kid really is the worst bully on the playground. Most people abandon the trail of evidence when they see it leading them somewhere they don't want to go, if they haven't already abandoned it because logic is such a burden. Flew, however, had spent a lifetime following evidence and was widely regarded as a fair-minded thinker. He would often, for example, acknowledge strengths in his opponent's arguments and weaknesses in his own. And he was cool-headed about it. Unlike the loud atheists that succeeded him—Richard Dawkins, Daniel Dennet, Jerry Coyne, Sam Harris, Christopher Hitchens—he was not inclined to ridicule or caricature those he disagreed with. His argument was not with his opponents; it was with their beliefs.

A trail of evidence began to appear in front of Flew, like the bread crumbs that Hansel and Gretel followed into the forest. He couldn't see clearly where the trail led, but, mindful of Socrates' wise counsel, he was determined to follow it.

BREAD CRUMBS LEADING TO GOD

For ever since the world was created, people have seen the earth and sky. Through everything God made, they can clearly see his invisible qualities—his eternal power and divine nature. So they have no excuse for not knowing God.

ROMANS 1:20

THREE TRAILS OF evidence attracted Flew's attention, all rooted in the scientific understanding of the world, for which he had great respect. The three trails are:

1. The remarkable character of the laws of nature that don't seem to be random features of the world or something that is self-explanatory.

2. The mysterious and subtle way that life originates from nonlife.

3. The unexplained origin of the world.

Flew's scientific breadcrumbs led him to new and surprising insights—at least new and surprising for him. He did not demolish all of the traditional objections to belief in God—he thought evil was still a problem, and that among the world religions there was still no good way to identify the right one. In fact, Flew did not really find religion at the end of his trail. Consistent with his commitment to follow the evidence as far as it led and no further, he stopped when the breadcrumbs ended. He did not complete his journey by making a leap of faith and returning to the Christianity of his childhood—a truly fairy-tale ending. But he did find, within science, evidence that compelled him to repudiate his lifelong atheism and embrace belief in God.

Figure 0.2. Antony Flew (1923-2010) was a British philosopher who taught at Oxford and the University of Aberdeen. He wrote and edited over thirty books including *The Presumption of Atheism* and *God: A Critical Inquiry*. (John Lawrence/www.johnlawrence.org.uk. Used by permission.)

Flew's journey is not all that remarkable however, for many great thinkers—C. S. Lewis and Francis Collins come to mind—have traveled that road from atheism to theism. It is a natural, although not required, journey for those who reflect on the deeper questions of existence. It is remarkable, however—and tragic—that so many of the

Figure 0.3. Antony Flew rejected atheism in the last decade of his life, penning a controversial confession that scholars continue to argue about. Some horrified atheists suggested he didn't really write it, but he disagreed!

former atheist's colleagues and fans concluded he must have either lost his mind along the way or had it hijacked by Christian apologists.[5]

Flew, like so many who ponder the depths of science, got caught up in the mysterious grandeur—the wonder—of the universe. This wonder points a finger beyond itself, calling for an explanation. Flew saw that finger pointing in the direction of God. "The heavens," as the psalmist wrote and the famous atheist came to appreciate at the dawn of the third millennium, "declare the glory of God" (Ps 19:1 NIV).

THE GLORY OF GOD

*Come, let's build a great city for ourselves with a tower that
reaches into the sky. This will make us famous and keep
us from being scattered all over the world.*

GENESIS 11:4

THE WONDER AND even the size of the universe that beckoned Flew has grown steadily for centuries. When the psalmist celebrated the heavens long before Christ, he had no idea how grand they were. His world was a tiny cardboard box compared to the one we understand today. His sky hung low overhead—an inverted bowl almost within reach—with stars fixed securely to it and windows to let in the rain and snow. Nevertheless, it was grand, as anyone who admires the night sky today understands and appreciates. In fact, the psalmist's sky was grander than ours, which is dulled by smog and light pollution, and competes with cable TV for our attention.

Christians over the centuries have added their voices to that of the psalmist. At least on camping trips, we still celebrate the heavens—and even more so now with our expanded appreciation for just how grand they are. Science has discovered so much that is wonderful about the world, and rather than fear that science threatens faith as so many do, we can rejoice in the scientific picture of the world, seeing it as the handiwork of our Creator.

The psalmist penned his celebration of the heavens in the Old Testament, long before the birth of science as we understand it today. Years earlier, after the great flood of Noah, in the plain of Shinar near modern-day Iraq, Genesis records that the children of Israel embarked on a most ambitious project—to build a tower "with its top in the heavens" (Gen 11). Such a project would make no sense today, of course, with our modern concept of the heavens (although we still build taller and taller buildings to show how important we are). But the tops of our tallest buildings today are not even close to being "in the heavens" (see center insert, figure A).

Ancient peoples perceived the sky to be very close overhead. The architects of the Tower of Babel believed they could construct a building that would reach into the heavens, where God resided.

The Tower of Babel and its ambitious agenda faded from the canvas of history almost three thousand years ago. Slowly we came to understand the scale of our world and the folly of constructing tall buildings to reach into the heavens. Now we send spaceships into the heavens, perhaps joining Babel's ancient architects in believing this gets us a bit closer to the gods.

Christians in the first millennium understood more about the heavens than the psalmist. They had the benefit of discoveries made by Greek thinkers in the centuries before Christ. The educated among them, like St. Augustine, knew the earth was round and not flat. It is a total myth, born of antireligious prejudice, that Christians used to think the earth was flat and persecuted those that thought otherwise. They even knew the size of the earth. Their sky was not a low tent roof, suspended over a flat earth, resting on the hills on the horizon—it was a glorious sphere, with the earth in the middle. They could see five planets with the naked eye—the telescope had not yet been invented—and there was no reason to suppose more existed. After all, they reasoned, God created the heavens for us to enjoy, and one can hardly enjoy looking at things they cannot see. There were roughly one thousand known stars, arranged in patterns that marked the seasons, and they were attached to a sphere just beyond the orbit of Saturn, the farthest planet.

This view of the heavens, which preceded the birth of Christianity, reigned without challenge into the sixteenth century and only slowly disappeared. It formed the backdrop for great Christian art and poetry, like Dante's *Divine Comedy* and Milton's *Paradise Lost*.

Upheaval, turmoil and adventure rocked the sixteenth century. Luther and other Reformers broke away from the Roman Catholic Church, splintering Christianity; European powers launched grand exploratory expeditions, colonizing and even enslaving people in far-off lands; global missions began in earnest as the gospel made its way around the world; new art forms exploded and science struggled to be born. Christian astronomers started to wonder and debate about whether the earth might move about the sun rather than the other way around. This dangerous proposition contradicted tradition and common sense—and likewise seemed to contradict a literal interpretation of the Bible, where we read in Psalm 93 that "the world stands firm and cannot be shaken." But the study of the natural world was considered appropriate for Christians, as a way to better understand God's creation.

The new "moving earth" astronomy eventually became quite controversial. Christians were divided on its plausibility. Nicolaus Copernicus, the Polish polymath who first proposed it, was a canon in the Roman Catholic Church and certainly not on any crusade to undermine the Bible or upset his fellow Christians. His contemporary Martin Luther rejected it and, in keeping with most educated people of his century, defended the traditional picture of the cosmos in his writings and lectures. A few decades later, the infamous Galileo Galilei accepted the radical new theory but got in trouble for promoting it too vigorously to a church that was not quite ready for prime-time astronomy.

Galileo was, as far as we know, the first person to use a telescope—just months after it was invented in Holland—to look more closely at the heavens. The enhanced view through his newly ground lenses inaugurated an explosive growth in our understanding of the grandeur of the heavens. Galileo's discoveries, in retrospect, seem bland—mountains on the moon, innumerably more stars overhead, small moons orbiting about Jupiter—but they created turmoil for those of his generation who were paying attention. The telescope had seemingly unlimited potential for improvement, and in tandem with steady advances in telescope technology the heavens opened up to eager astronomers like the front gates of Disney World open every morning for children in search of adventure.

New planets were discovered—Uranus in 1781, Neptune in 1846, and Pluto in 1930 (although poor Pluto, with much wailing and gnashing of teeth from its groupies, was kicked out of the planetary club in 2006). The number

Figure 0.4. Sketch from Martin Luther's Bible, first printed in 1534 while Copernicus was working on his famous book. The illustration shows a cosmos with everything orbiting about the earth. The image of "waters above" comes from the creation story in Genesis 1:6-10 where God is described as separating the waters below from those that are above. The English text was, obviously, not in Martin Luther's Bible but was a later addition. (Hans Lufft/Wikimedia Commons)

of visible stars increased with each improvement in the telescope. Puzzling and unfamiliar structures that resembled globs of cotton candy came into view. The eighteenth-century philosopher Immanuel Kant called them "Island Universes," arguing that our sun was simply one star in the Milky Way galaxy, and these other globs—some of which had interesting spiral structures—were other galaxies, but so far away we couldn't make out individual stars. His skeptical detractors said the globs were just cosmic dust bunnies. Kant, one of the greatest thinkers of his time, would later reflect that "Two things fill the mind with ever new and increasing admiration and awe: the starry heavens above me and the moral law within."[6] The heavens above and the moral law within emerged as important and enduring themes in Kant's century, as Christians began to think about the significance of the "book of nature" and the "book of conscience" as volumes supplementing the "book of Scripture."

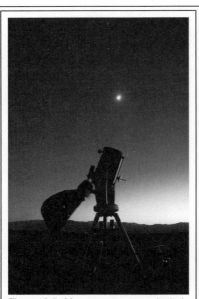

Figure 0.5. Many astronomers, including my former student Stephanie Capen (pictured here with her telescope), are looking for earthlike "exoplanets" outside our solar system in hopes of finding life. These planets orbiting stars light years away (trillions of miles). Current instrumentation is not sensitive enough to detect such small earthlike planets directly, so astronomers seek indirect methods. Capen worked on Transit-Timing Variation, with Dr. Nader Haghighipour at the University of Hawaii, and helped show that this technique would indeed be capable of detecting earthlike planets around other stars. (Used courtesy of Alexander Savello)

In the early decades of the twentieth century, astronomers discovered many of Kant's island universes. New techniques were developed to estimate how far away these galaxies were and three-dimensional maps of the heavens were constructed. These maps were like the maps of the ancient world that always had significant swaths of terra incognita—unknown territory on the edges of the most recent exploration. Just as sailors in the sixteenth century would venture ever farther from home as they explored planet earth, so the astronomers advanced their technology to reach farther out into space to push back the envelope of the cosmic terra incognita.

Ingenious new technologies make it possible to "see" the universe in new ways. We now have telescopes that look for radio waves, gamma rays and x-rays. Radiation from the ultraviolet and infrared parts of the spectrum can be detected with new technologies. We have techniques for determining if a distant star has a planet around it by looking at tiny wobbles in the path of the star through space. One of my students, Stephanie Capen, spent the summer of her junior year working in an observatory in Hawaii making measurements to determine whether distant stars have planets, which cannot be seen directly against the glare of the star they are orbiting.

We can identify the chemical composition of much of the universe. We see unmistakable evidence that distant stars are made of hydrogen and helium, atoms that exist in abundance here on earth. The old nursery rhyme "Twinkle, twinkle, little star, How I wonder what you are" is obsolete. We know exactly what the stars are. We can see that the stars are arranged in galaxies, often resembling our own Milky Way. The galaxies, despite their vast size—most contain hundreds of billions of stars—are themselves gathered into clusters of galaxies, just as large cities are clustered on the northeastern seaboard of the United States.

The universe that inspired the psalmist three thousand years ago grows grander as each new generation of astronomers adds yet another layer of understanding. Each new discovery pushes back the boundary that separates the known universe from the vast terra incognita that beckons and teases us to keep going, to sail ever further from familiar shores.

THE WONDER OF THE WORLD

Two things fill the mind with ever new and increasing admiration and awe, the more often and steadily reflection is occupied with them: the starry heaven above me and the moral law within me. Neither of them need I seek and merely suspect as if shrouded in obscurity or rapture beyond my own horizon; I see them before me and connect them immediately with my existence.

IMMANUEL KANT

THE NIGHT SKY still beckons us, as it once did the psalmist. I spend time each summer at a rustic family cottage in the wilderness of my

Figure 0.6. The night sky, when observed without the interference of artificial light or smog, is spectacular. Here we can see a couple of "shooting stars" against the panorama of the rich background of stars. Shooting stars are remarkably misnamed. They are not stars at all, but small meteoroids burning up as they enter the earth's atmosphere at great speeds. But, even though they are in the earth's atmosphere, they appear to be as far away as the stars. (Used courtesy of Tom Oord)

native New Brunswick, Canada. There, miles from electricity, the night sky does not compete with artificial light. Smog does not obscure it. Planes do not draw white trails on it. It does not compete with cable television or even cell phones, silenced by the absence of signals. The night sky is simply there, quietly declaring the glory of God. Its many lights reflect off the ripples of the lake, and are accompanied by the rustling of leaves and the voices of the many creatures that call this wilderness home. Only a jaded soul could sit by that lake and not wonder if there wasn't some larger meaning to the experience.

I can see what the psalmist saw and rejoice as he did. But I watch the night sky through the eyes of a twenty-first-century scientist. I have the benefit of centuries of scientific advancement and can see, in my mind's eye, so much more. Those visible stars are just the advance guard of a virtually infinite army of stars going back almost forever. The stars are not attached to a dome that one might reach with an ambitiously tall tower or puncture with a long-range missile. They are so far away that their light has been traveling at unimaginable speed for years, centuries, millennia and longer. The light from the stars in the Hyades Cluster began its journey to the earth at about the time that my ancestors—Loyalists from Pennsylvania—began their journey to this part of North America in the eighteenth century. The light from the closest stars, the trio that make up Alpha Centauri, takes over four years to reach earth. The most distant star ever detected from the earth is a "gamma ray burster" that launched its signal almost 13 billion years ago, when the universe was young. The powerful gamma ray signal from this star began its journey before our planet was even formed, reaching the earth in April 2009.[7]

The psalmist did not know that the stars were made of hydrogen and helium. He did not know they generated their energy through nuclear fusion or that many of them explode at the end of their lives. He knew nothing of galaxies and the layers of structure in the cosmos. He did not understand how fast light travels or that the light from our sun powers photosynthesis and many other processes here on the earth.

The universe brought into view by science is like a collection of Russian matryoshka dolls nestled one inside the other. With the psalmist we can see the outer layer—and it is grand. But inside are additional layers, each one with a new type of grandeur. And at the very end of the unpacking lie the remarkable laws of physics that keep the earth orbiting about the sun, the sun shining reliably, and the sunlight providing energy to sustain life on our planet.

The universe as we understand it today inspires awe. And for those open to its message—from the psalmists of yesteryear to the believers and even the thoughtful skeptics of today—it speaks of a Creator. Our universe does not look like a cosmic accident, where lots of stuff just happened. It looks like the expression of a grand plan—a cosmic architecture capable of both supporting life such as ours and of inspiring observers like us to seek out the Creator.

This is why Antony Flew—"world's most notorious atheist"—changed his mind and started believing in God.

In the pages that follow I want to share this story with you. We live in a world of wonder. Only the flattest of lukewarm souls is not moved by the grandeur of our universe. Most of us find the universe truly awesome. And, while not everyone comes to believe in a Creator, there are few that can simply shrug their shoulders and set aside the mystery of our existence. Looked at in the right way, the modern scientific picture draws us ever deeper into this wonder, into the mind of the Creator.

1

LEARNING TO READ
THE BOOK OF NATURE

The Beginning of Science

Father and son flew side by side,
Free as birds, belying their fate.
Far from their prison, its solemn walls,
Adieu, accursed land of Crete!

PRATYUSH TIWARI

ONCE UPON A TIME A CLEVER Greek craftsman named Daedalus got in trouble with the king. He and his son, Icarus, were exiled to Crete and imprisoned. Daedalus naturally wanted to escape, so he ingeniously arranged that he and his son would fly off the island like birds. He gathered feathers and stuck them together with wax, making wings for the two of them to fly.

Before they took off on their escape, Daedalus anticipated the problems they would encounter. He warned Icarus, for example, not to fly too close to the sun lest its heat melt the wax holding together the feathers in his wings.

Icarus and Daedalus took off to freedom, experiencing what many humans only dream about—flying in the air like a bird, unfettered from gravity, swooping, circling and cruising above the earth, looking down on everything below. Icarus found flying exhilarating and soon forgot that he was flying to freedom and escaping from exile. He got carried away by his new ability to fly, like a superhero first discovering his powers, or Harry Potter discovering he can do magic. Caught up in the moment, giddy with excitement, Icarus forgot all about his father and the sober advice he had given. He flew higher and higher, circling at ever greater heights. Each passing moment found him farther from the lowly altitudes and earthly constraints that once bound him. He had become a birdman, freed from the leash of gravity that kept lesser mortals plastered to the ground. He was more free than he had ever been.

Eventually Icarus began to descend and found himself unable to stop. In vain he flapped his wings harder and harder until he realized that he had no wings. Forgetting his father's advice, the hapless Icarus had flown too close to the sun, and the heat melted the wax. His powers of flight were gone and he was no longer a birdman. He was back to being a mere human, albeit one unfortunately located high in the sky, covered in melting wax, but without wings. The surface of the earth, from which he had celebrated his liberation just moments earlier, rushed to meet him as he spent his final seconds of freedom plummeting to his death. He fell into the water in an area that is now called the Icarian Sea, southwest of the island of Samos.

Figure 1.1. The Icarian Sea, where the mythological Icarus is said to have plummeted to his death after the nearby sun melted the wax that held his wings on. Ancient cosmologies generally assumed the sun was very close. (Pieter Bruegel the Elder/Wikimedia Commons)

The mythological tale of Icarus endures as a colorful warning not to lose contact with reality, lifted by pride to exalted heights from which one cannot help but fall.

Pride, they say always hath a fall,
And so it was, Icarus fell.
From the warmth of blazing Apollo,
To the cold where mermaids dwell.[1]

A more mundane lesson can be learned from the story of Icarus. Such mythological tales take place within framework of the real world, as understood by the mythmakers. There is, for example, an Icarian Sea, and one can sail there and view the spot where Daedalus's proud son is said to have plummeted to his death. The story of Icarus also illuminates the worldview of the ancient Greeks. Recall Daedalus's warning not to fly too near the sun. This obscure part of the story is never emphasized for the obvious reason that it is not the point and not even related to the point.

The Greeks—Daedalus, Icarus and everyone from that era—had a completely wrong idea about where the sun was. They thought the sun was so close that flying high above the earth would place one closer to it in some meaningful sense. Let us think about this.

The sun is 93 million miles away. Even if poor Icarus flew to an altitude equal to the peak of Mount Everest—just under six miles high and far beyond what a Mediterranean native could have imagined—he would still be less than a tiny fraction of 1 percent closer to the sun than he would be at sea level. The intensity of the sun's rays would not be noticeably stronger at that "closer" distance. And, of course, the dangers at that height come from thin air and cold temperatures, not proximity to the sun.

The story of Icarus provides a fascinating insight into the cosmology

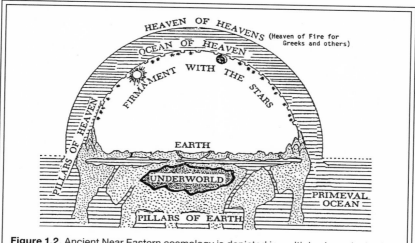

Figure 1.2. Ancient Near Eastern cosmology is depicted in multiple places in the Old Testament. The firmament was believed to be a solid dome overhead that could hold back the heavenly waters.

of the ancient world—they thought the sun was right above their heads. It was a widespread belief, seemingly held by all civilizations. The Egyptians thought the sky was a sort of tent canopy, supported by the mountains at the four corners of the earth. The solid sky, across which the sun moved every day, was not much higher than the modestly proportioned mountains they saw on the horizon. Ancient Chinese astronomers made their observations from the top of modest stone buildings called ziggurats, believing they had climbed a bit closer to the stars and should be able to see them better. The Tower of Babel was intended to have its "top in the heavens" which, taken at face value, would imply that one could step off the top of the tower onto the moon.

These ancient worldviews are sometimes lampooned and their architects dismissed as clueless simpletons trapped in a Mother Goose reality. Such judgments are unfair, for their worldviews were, quite simply, straightforward naked-eye constructions. If you look closely at the night sky you will see exactly what they saw (although pollution and artificial lights will diminish your view). Stand under the stars on a clear night and look up, forgetting how many Star Trek movies you have seen. You will clearly see a dome above your head with stars attached to it. The stars give the unmistakable impression that they are all the same distance away. The ones on the horizon do not look far from the mountains, which are just beneath them. The reality, as we know, is dramatically different, but it sure doesn't look that way.

Take the Big Dipper as an example. The stars in that familiar constellation are at very different distances from the earth. The star on the tip of the handle, for example, is trillions of miles farther away than the stars at the bottom of the bowl part of the constellation. And yet, when we look at it with the naked eye, we see that set of stars as part of a common pattern, like numbered dots on a page to be connected.

Today we ridicule the idea of a flat earth. We imagine the Flat Earth Society as a collection of silly illiterates—Flintstones—with worldviews left over from the Stone Age. A flat earth with a dome of stars overhead, however, is actually a commonsense inference from simple everyday observations. And, of course, the sky looked just as grand to the flat-earthers of yesteryear as it does to us today.

The contrast between the natural appearance of the world and its scientific description is striking. But we must take note of it or we do a great disservice to those who lived in centuries past. The biblical authors, for example, described the world as it appeared to them, in the language and concepts of their culture. They spoke, for example, of sunrise and sunset because those were important parts of their day. Even now we use these concepts, implicitly acknowledging that often the appearance of the world is more relevant to us than the reality.

Our appreciation of the world is made even more wondrous, of course, by the many great discoveries of science that have revealed so much more about the creation. But these discoveries are not visible to the naked eye.

That is the theme of this book—that our expanding view of the world around us provides us with a constant new source of wonder that motivates reflection on the Creator of this world.

ROUNDING OUT THE EARTH

Never in all their history have men been able truly to conceive of the world as one: a single sphere, a globe, having the qualities of a globe, a round earth in which all the directions eventually meet, in which there is no center because every point, or none, is center—an equal earth which all men occupy as equals. The airman's earth, if free men make it, will be truly round: a globe in practice, not in theory.

ARCHIBALD MACLEISH

A FEW CENTURIES before Christ the Greeks figured out that the earth is round, a giant leap forward. Around 500 B.C. Pythagoras—of the beloved math theorem about triangles—thought long and hard about the odd appearance of the moon as it went through its phases. The line separating the dark and light parts of the moon had an interesting shape that could be explained only by assuming that the moon was round. Pythagoras then took a speculative leap and concluded that the earth must be the same shape as the moon (see insert figure B).

Within a century, another Greek, Anaxagoras, figured out what eclipses were. In particular he noted that the shadow cast by the earth on the moon during a lunar eclipse was round—therefore the earth must be round. These were just more sophisticated naked-eye observations, but Greek philosophers were a speculative bunch with time on their hands—thanks to a generous allotment of slaves who looked after them—and often pushed past the most immediate visual impressions. By 350 B.C. there was a consensus that the earth is a sphere. Aristotle noted that seafaring travelers reported seeing different constellations as they traveled farther and farther from the equator. The Southern Cross constellation, for example, dominates the night sky in the southern hemisphere, but can barely be seen from above the equator and never seen as far north as Boston, where I live.

Aristotle and others developed convincing arguments for the shape of the earth, and in the centuries that followed virtually no educated thinker familiar with the arguments rejected them in favor of the old idea that the earth was flat. In fact, from the time of Christ to the scientific revolution of Isaac Newton in the seventeenth century, we know of only two thinkers who rejected the idea that the earth was a sphere. One was a minor figure in early Christianity, St. Lactantius (c. 240-c. 325); the other was an eccentric sixth-century geographer named Cosmas, who

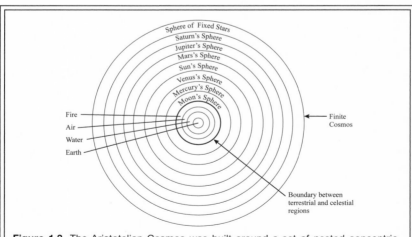

Figure 1.3. The Aristotelian Cosmos was built around a set of nested concentric spheres. The model was both aesthetically beautiful and explanatory. Almost everything that could be observed in the heavens was explained very simply with this model, which is why it has lasted for two thousand years.

argued that the Bible taught that the world was flat and the heavens form a curved lid above it. He produced illustrations of this flat earth based on Hebrews 9:1-5, where we read that the "earthly sanctuary" must resemble the ancient tabernacle of Moses. As far as we can tell, nobody agreed with this hyper-literal reading of Hebrews. Many thought it was absurd. Of course this has not stopped antireligious polemicists from claiming it was *the* Christian view in the first millennium.[2] No evidence exists, however, that the early church thought the earth was flat, despite the occasional biblical reference to the earth having "corners" or other everyday expressions of the sort that we still use.

Not long after Aristotle, other Greeks, convinced that the earth was a sphere, developed ingenious geometrical techniques to estimate the size of the earth and got it essentially correct. The shape and size of the earth created a starting point for a model of the universe that would last until the time of Galileo and Newton. This geocentric (earth-centered) model placed the known planets—Mercury, Venus, Mars, Jupiter, Saturn—on solid transparent spheres arranged concentrically about the earth and attached all the known stars—about a thousand—to a huge sphere not far beyond Saturn. This starry sphere was essentially the solid sky of the ancients stretched all the way around an earth that was now viewed as spherical rather than flat. The transparent spheres were said to be made of a crystalline material called *ether*—a "heavenly" material not found on the earth.

UNHOOKING THE EARTH

And new Philosophy calls all in doubt,
The element of fire is quite put out;
The Sun is lost, and the earth, and no man's wit
Can well direct him where to look for it.

JOHN DONNE

THE EARTH-CENTERED UNIVERSE played a central role in the developing worldview of the Christian tradition and figures prominently in much of the art, poetry, philosophy and theology of the medieval and Renaissance periods. In the medieval version of the solar system, hell was at the center of the creation, surrounded by an earth groaning under the curse of sin and home to troubled souls living in a vale of tears. As we went out from the earth, though, things got better until we reached the heavens, which were perfect. This highly geometrical model, constructed of perfect circles and incorruptible ether, was rich in theological symbolism, as befitted a system originating in the mind of God.

This elegant system was destined to be replaced through the work of four remarkable thinkers: Nicolaus Copernicus, Johannes Kepler, Galileo Galilei and Isaac Newton. All four of these thinkers—two Catholics and two Protestants—were fully convinced that God had created the world and they were thinking his thoughts after him, even if those thoughts seemed less godly than their predecessors. All of them wrestled with the religious implications of their ideas, not so much for themselves, though, as for others who found the changes threatening. They were captivated by the wonder of coming to a greater understanding of God's creation and convinced they could see an even deeper expression of God's handiwork in the world they were explaining.

The revolution began in 1543 with Copernicus, a canon in the Roman Catholic Church in Poland. He reasoned, logically enough, that if the prevailing model for the heavens was indeed the handiwork of God, then it ought to work better. Calendars based on it should not become useless so quickly, and the constellations marking the seasons should show up on time. "I began to be annoyed," he wrote from his posting in a remote part of Poland, "that the philosophers had discovered no sure scheme for the movements of the machinery of the world, created for our sake by the best and most systematic Artist of all."[3]

Emboldened by this frustration, he unhooked the earth and placed it in the heavens. Things began to make more sense with this model, although why the fallen and corrupt earth should be in the heavens remained a mystery. His book *On the Revolutions of the Heavenly Spheres* laid out for the first time the reasons why a geometrical model with the sun at the center and the earth moving about it made more sense than a model with the earth at the center. The idea was not entirely original, but Copernicus was the first to work out the details.

The moving earth was a problem, however, troubling his critics

Figures 1.4-7. The revolution in astronomy was led by four Christian thinkers, two Protestant and two Catholic: (clockwise beginning in upper left) Copernicus (1473-1543), Kepler (1571-1630), Galileo (1564-1642) and Newton (1643-1727). (Kepler: Wikimedia Commons; Copernicus, Galileo and Newton: Used by permission. ©Georgios Kollidas/depositphotos)

and anyone who thought carefully about it. Nobody could imagine an earth turning on its axis so fast that its surface was moving at a thousand miles per hour, or hurtling through space in its orbit around the sun at almost seventy thousand miles per hour. Surely such dramatic motions would have *some* noticeable effects—like a steady wind or a tendency for falling objects to come back to a different spot than they were launched from.

Galileo, a brilliant Italian Catholic and one of the first converts to the Copernican model, worked out the physics of a moving earth, clarifying ambiguities and explaining why things thrown straight up fell back to where they started rather than to a distant spot as the earth moved out from under it, like someone throwing a baseball up through the sunroof of a speeding car.

Galileo also refined the telescope and made several discoveries that convinced him that the received medieval wisdom about astronomy was all wrong. One convinced him that the moon was just like the earth and not a special "heavenly" body as everyone had assumed. Another convinced him that there were many more stars than anyone had thought, and they were distributed through the depths of space, not all attached to a sphere just beyond Saturn. His discoveries came so fast and furious that he was sure God must have anointed him, or at least his new telescope, with some sort of heavenly oil. "I render infinite thanks to God," he declared piously, "for being so kind as to make me alone the first observer of marvels kept hidden in obscurity for all previous centuries."[4]

Kepler, a German Lutheran and deeply spiritual Christian who once had to interrupt his research to defend his mother against charges of witchcraft, showed that the planets did not move in the perfect circles long assigned to them. Their orbits were ellipses. And they sped up when they got closer to the sun and slowed down when they were farther away, puzzling behavior for heavenly bodies not allowed to change in any way.

Like Galileo, Kepler saw his work as a form of worship, a new way to appreciate his Creator. "I give thanks, Creator and Lord, that thou allowest me to rejoice in thy works," Kepler wrote in a prayer still being quoted. "Praise the Lord ye heavenly harmonies, and ye who know the heavenly harmonies."[5]

Kepler tried without success to explain the very different motion of the planets that he had discovered. Intuitively he was sure the sun must be exerting some kind of force on the planets, but he couldn't quite put it all together. That task, which would turn out to be the grand finale of the conversation started by Copernicus, was accomplished by Isaac Newton, born prematurely on Christmas Day 1642, the year of Galileo's death.

Newton cued off Galileo's discovery that the bodies in the heavens seemed much like the bodies on the earth. If true, then maybe the earth reaches out into space and pulls on the moon, just as it pulls on everything on the earth, like the fictitious apple that fell on his head.

Newton's speculation turned out to be correct. The result was the law of gravity—a remarkable and wide-ranging explanation for almost everything going on in the heavens. No longer would anyone need to wonder if angels were pushing the planets around in their orbits, or if there was some mysterious heavenly power "up there" with no analog on the earth. As for why the earth belonged in the perfect heavens—it turned out the heavens were not so perfect after all, and hell was not in the center of the earth. There was, said Newton, just one glorious universe going on forever with the same laws of physics working everywhere. And, of course, it was the handiwork of God—one supremely rational being who would certainly create a universe with the same laws operating throughout.

"This most beautiful system of the sun, planets, and comets," he wrote at the end of his greatest work,

> could only proceed from the counsel and dominion of an intelligent and powerful Being. And if the fixed stars are the centres of other like systems, these, being formed by the like wise counsel, must be all subject to the dominion of One; especially since the light of the fixed stars is of the same nature with the light of the sun, and from every system light passes into all the other systems: and lest the systems of the fixed stars should, by their gravity, fall on each other, he hath placed those systems at immense distances from one another.[6]

THE BOOK OF NATURE

Take note, theologians, that in your desire to make matters of faith
out of propositions relating to the fixity of sun and earth you run the risk
of eventually having to condemn as heretics those who would declare the earth
to stand still and the sun to change position—eventually, I say, at such
a time as it might be physically or logically proved that
the earth moves and the sun stands still.

GALILEO

COPERNICUS, GALILEO, KEPLER, NEWTON and their many colleagues opened up and began to read the "Book of Nature," a metaphor inviting comparison with the "Book of Scripture," which was important to all of them, as deeply committed Christians. The arrival of the book of nature, which would eventually be called "science" was significant. It meant that humans could actually "read" the natural world. We take this for granted today since we have been doing it for centuries, but it is far from obvious why we should be able to understand the world. Einstein commented near the end of his life that the "the eternal mystery of the universe is that it is comprehensible."[7]

It was far from clear when Copernicus began his work just how much humans should expect to understand about the world. We were fallen creatures, but created in the image of God. Did the divine flame still flicker within us, allowing us to think God's thoughts after him? Or was the world an eternal mystery, inaccessible to our investigation, as weather patterns would appear to our dogs?

Suddenly we had all these new truths about the world that God had created. The author of the book of nature was God, and these early scientists were deciphering the language used by God. Galileo even used the language metaphor to explain why the truths being discovered in the new "philosophy," as it was called then, should be placed on the same playing field as the truths of the Bible, which revealed a different and complementary type of truth.

Philosophy is written in that great book which ever lies before our eyes—I mean the universe—but we cannot understand it if we do not first learn the language and grasp the symbols in which it is written. This book is written in mathematical language, and the symbols are triangles, circles and other geometrical figures, without whose help it is humanly impossible to comprehend a single word of it, and without which one wanders in vain though a dark labyrinth.[8]

We call the period from Copernicus to Newton the "Scientific Revolution." It witnessed the birth not only of a new model for the solar system but of modern science itself. Galileo's comments about the language of mathematics described the science struggling to be born in a world where truth was more typically thought to reside in ancient traditions and texts and not in theories about natural phenomena. Mathematical models of physical reality were appearing, through a glass darkly, but growing ever clearer—almost like an unfolding revelation. These models would allow scientists to understand, at the deepest level, the source of order in the world. This order, as they contemplated it, came straight from the mind of God, an affirmation that permeates their writings.

The rather sudden emergence of modern science in Western Europe has long fascinated scholars intrigued by its uniqueness. Asian and Islamic cultures were more advanced at the time, but science did not emerge there and had to be imported sometime later. An interesting case can be made that Christianity played a central role in the origin of science. Western Europe was, of course, deeply Christian. The Roman Catholic Church had long provided whatever educational structures were available, and many leading scholars, like Copernicus, were in the employ of the church. Protestantism continued this emphasis. Every one of Newton's professors at Cambridge University, for example, was ordained in the Church of England, regardless of the subject taught. But more significantly Christianity had developed a deep and profound theology of creation that saw the world as having been *freely created by a rational God.* There were two parts to this belief. In the first place, the world was *rational.* Its behavior was more like that of an orderly machine rather than a living creature with an inscrutable free will. It was thus possible, in principle, to reverse engineer the world and see how it was put together, in the same way that an old-fashioned clock could be dismantled to see how it worked. In the second place, God had created *freely*, which meant that the creation was not simply the expression of preexisting timeless rational structures. If it was, then it might be possible to merely *think* about how things should be. Instead, scientists would have to *inspect* the world empirically to see what it was like. God freely created patterns of rationality in nature—patterns only discernable through *observation*. There is no way to know exactly where people like Galileo and Newton got their intuitions about how to do science. But it is certainly true that what they were doing was profoundly consistent with their theology, and there is reason to believe their theology actually motivated their work.

Once the new science took root and began to grow, there was no turning back. Between rapid advances in telescopes, to which both Galileo and Newton contributed, and the steady extension and improvement of theoretical ideas like gravity and energy, a steady forward progression of our understanding of the natural world began. No longer would simple observations generate enduring models of the universe that would last for two thousand years.

2

A WONDERFUL WORLD

Science Learns to Walk

Science is young. Whether it will survive long enough to become old depends upon our sanity and courage and vigor, and, as one always must add in this nuclear age, upon whether we blow ourselves up first.

TIMOTHY FERRIS

SCIENCE, ONCE IT LEARNED TO WALK, marched forward. It started walking in the seventeenth century and like a toddler moved unsteadily at first, in fits and starts. Also like a toddler, science walks on two legs. The first leg is that of *observation*, and all scientific progress begins when we notice something interesting. As technology improved, producing better telescopes and microscopes than the primitive spyglasses that launched Galileo's career, we simply saw things that we could not have seen before. The second leg science walks on is that of explanation or *theory*. A theory is an explanation that scientists have developed that makes sense of observations. The best-known example is Newton's theory of gravity, which explained why the planets remained tethered to the sun and why they moved in their particular paths.

Theory is a widely misused term in our conversation today, creating much confusion about the nature of science. Most people equate theory with *guess*. We hear things like, "My theory is that the next terrorist attack will be in Washington, D.C.," or "My theory is that the government knows aliens landed in 1947 and is covering it up." This use of the word *theory* has nothing to do with the way scientists use it. In fact, this common use is what a scientist would call a "guess" or at best a "hypothesis," which is an educated guess. A theory is a wide-ranging explanation for many observations that has been tested many times. Newton's theory of gravity was hardly a guess. It was a comprehensive mathematical explanation for how things fall—*all* things, not just one or two. In fact most theories, as the term is used in science, including Newton's famous theory of gravity, took considerable effort—and a lot of creativity—to "find," and even more effort to check carefully against observation en route to concluding the theory was true.

But the discovery of a theory is not like the discovery of a new planet or a continent. Columbus and his crew blundered into North America as a consequence of making the worst geographical miscalculation in history. Theories require imagination and creativity—sometimes in great quantities. Newton's insight that the earth's ghostly fingers of gravity could reach out through empty space and tug on the moon did not leap out of the equations on the page in front of him. It required a confident creativity to even contemplate that possibility. Science resembles art in the way it feeds on fresh new ideas.

Scientific explorations are not always successful, of course, and it took some years for Newton's inspired explanation to pass enough tests to silence the skeptics. When the dust had settled, Newton's work on gravity accomplished two things: (1) It provided an explanation for the motions of bodies in the heavens—an explanation that became increasingly powerful as it was extended to more and more of the universe. (2) The stunning and far-reaching success of the explanation suggested that the world was not an impenetrable mystery. Scientists were inspired to look for—and find—explanatory theories to account for everything from the frequency of the tides to the changing of the seasons and the twinkling of the stars. Our picture of the universe steadily improved. Science was up and running, and there was no looking back to a bygone era when it seemed like human beings were simply not capable of understanding the mysterious world around them.

THE BROAD WHITE ROAD IN HEAVEN

Many things Nokomis taught him
Of the stars that shine in heaven;
Showed him Ishkoodah, the comet,
Ishkoodah, with fiery tresses; . . .
Showed the broad white road in heaven,
Pathway of the ghosts, the shadows,
Running straight across the heavens,
Crowded with the ghosts, the shadows.

HENRY WADSWORTH LONGFELLOW

FOR DECADES AFTER Newton stepped down from his pinnacle atop the new world of science, our skyward gaze reached further and further out into the heavens, like a extendable telescope getting longer and longer. If there be any truth in the expression "There is nothing new *under* the sun," there was certainly no truth at all to the venerable claim that there could be nothing new *beyond* the sun. Telescopes and even careful naked-eye observations revealed much that was new. The white swath of stars in the heavens—Hiawatha's "broad white road"—was found to be a gigantic disk of stars—the galaxy we now call the Milky Way. Cloudy white globs in the night sky were discovered to be other galaxies beyond our own, raising provocative questions about the size of the universe.

Closer to home, new planets were discovered—first Uranus, then Neptune and Pluto. Eventually planets would be discovered beyond our solar system, leading to speculation that the universe might be teeming with life. New comets were discovered. Once thought to be astrological messengers of doom, comets had been tamed by Newton's friend Edmund Halley. Using the new theory of gravity he calculated the path of a comet based on a bold assumption that the comets that had previously appeared in 1531, 1607 and 1682 were actually just the same comet making seventy-six-year-long rounds. Halley predicted the comet would reappear in 1758, and sure enough it showed up as predicted. The explanatory powers of science grew steadily.

Gradually the heavens were demystified—in part—as our telescopes and theories reached farther into space, seeing more and explaining more. Our remarkable planet is a tiny speck orbiting 93 million miles from an unremarkable but very reliable star we call the sun. The earth is one of eight planets and countless other smaller bodies, including poor demoted Pluto, still orbiting about the sun despite having been kicked out of the planet club.

The gravitational pull of the sun gets steadily weaker as we move out through the solar system and the orbiting bodies go slower and slower. Mercury, closest to the sun races around in eighty-eight days at a speed of thirty miles per second.[1] The earth, of course, takes a year and Pluto takes 248 years.[2] The slowest bodies in the solar system are way beyond Pluto in what is called the Oort cloud. Those distant suburbs are populated by comets and related objects that take thousands of years to complete their leisurely stroll about the sun.[3]

The distances in our solar system are unimaginably vast. A trip around the earth, as a starting point for comparison, is 25,000 miles, a typical odometer reading on a two-year-old car.[4] The nearest object to us is, of course, the moon, just under 240,000 miles away, which is about equal to the odometer reading on an old car.[5] It took the Apollo spacecraft three days to travel to the moon, our closest neighbor.[6] The sun, far from being just over our heads as Icarus, Daedalus and the architects at Babel thought, is 93 million miles away. It takes light eight minutes, twenty seconds to get from the sun to the earth, traveling at the breakneck speed of 186,000 miles per second. The closest planet to us is Mars, 34 million miles away at its closest point and 249 million miles at its furthest.[7] NASA is discussing a mission that would take astronauts to Mars for the first time. Even with careful planning to make the trip as short as possible, estimates are that the trip would take two and a half years.[8] A modest lobby has emerged that this need not be a round trip: NASA should send volunteers to colonize Mars with no plan to return, not unlike many of the adventures that brought Europeans to North America with little chance they could return.

Mars, of course, is the "planet next door." Ex-planet Pluto is 2.75 billion miles from earth at the closest point.[9] The Oort cloud, however, contains cometlike objects an unimaginable 18 trillion miles from the earth.[10] It takes over three years for light to travel from the bodies in the Oort cloud to the earth.[11] The material in the cloud spreads over a gigantic largely unmapped sphere centered on the sun, a sort of messy twenty-first-century version of the sphere of stars that everyone from Aristotle to Copernicus thought was fixed about the central, stationary earth.

Our solar system, in all likelihood, is as much of the universe as we could ever explore physically, even with great improvements in technology and substantial advances in the space program. In fact, it is all but inconceivable that we could even explore beyond our planetary system. Given the heroic efforts being considered to travel the short hop to Mars, it is difficult to imagine an expedition beyond, as least one that would carry people. The barriers that make space travel so challenging are not primarily technological, although it would be great if they were. The challenges have to do with basic science: There is simply no way to travel billions of miles in a reasonable amount of time. The "warp engines" on the starship Enterprise, essential for the Star Trek world so the crew can "boldly go where no one has gone before," are not on the drawing board at NASA. They are science fiction. Without a science-fiction engine, the crew could at best "boldly go just slightly beyond where we have been already."

Such limitations are sobering, even frustrating. We have learned so much about our universe, and one of those things is that we are destined to be a local species, forever constrained to our solar system. We can visit the moon, put space stations in orbit about the earth, perhaps even colonize Mars. Maybe, in the distant future we could visit one of the moons of Jupiter that Galileo discovered. But the great ships of exploration will not carry us to new worlds beyond those in our backyard.

Unmanned missions, in contrast, have traveled through our solar system, although they can't go much farther in any meaningful sense. The most successful were Voyager 1 and 2, which took breathtakingly beautiful pictures of the planets as they passed them. The most provocative image of all, however, was that of earth taken by Voyager 1 from the outer reaches of the solar system.[12] The camera was directed to look out the "back window" of the spaceship, toward the inner solar system it had left behind months earlier. There, in blackness so dark, across an expanse so vast that even the sun seemed but a candle in a distant window, was a tiny dot—our planetary home.

The picture of our planet from such a perspective is provocative and sobering. On that tiny dot we call home are several billion human beings. Very few of them think about the fragility of their planetary home or their responsibility as stewards. Instead, some of them fret about their property lines, worried that their neighbor is encroaching on their land. Machines dig huge holes and carry rocks from one part of the dot to another. Tiny ribbons of asphalt crisscross the dot, and planes carry people on "long" journeys from one side of the dot to the other. Weapons of mass destruction sit poised and ready to launch from secret locations—weapons with the collective power to wipe out all life on the dot and make it as sterile and uninhabitable as the cold-hearted orb that rules its night.

What are we to make of this perspective? Seventeenth-century Christians pondered the significance of the new model for the solar system that placed their home in the unreachable heavens. Now it seems we have been put back—and not even at the center of anything (see insert figure C). But this is not the best way to look at it, as we will see in chapter five.

MUCH ADO ABOUT NEXT TO NOTHING

So, naturalists observe, a flea
Has smaller fleas that on him prey;
And these have smaller still to bite 'em;
And so proceed ad infinitum.

JONATHAN SWIFT

IN TERMS OF size, our planet is nothing of consequence—a dust mote suspended in light rays from a distant and unremarkable star. Of course, size is hardly an adequate criterion to evaluate significance, but it seems we never get over our childhood intuition that to be "bigger" is somehow better. Toddlers are quite pleased to be told they are "big kids." And even adults are statistically more likely to vote for tall politicians or disrespect short people. This intuition about the relevance of size is depressing when we think about the earth in space. The earth, in the context of our solar system, is indeed a dot—less than the period at the end of a sentence. But it gets worse. Our solar system, in its larger context, is also a dot.

Our sun is but one of some 200 billion stars in the Milky Way galaxy—200 *billion*, not million. That vast sphere centered on the sun and reaching to the Oort cloud is just one solar system. The Milky Way is a flattened assemblage of stars with spiral arms spinning slowly. To the naked eye it can appear like a glowing white smear across the night sky—Hiawatha's "broad white road."

The Milky Way galaxy presents us with an unimaginably greater set of distances, like a child first discovering that there is a world outside of his neighborhood, on the other side of his or her own big front lawn. Those vast distances within our solar system that we can never traverse are all contained within a tiny speck within our galaxy. Each star, to the best of our knowledge, may have its own system of satellites orbiting about it, a system that may be more or less like our solar system— we just don't know, except in rare cases (see insert figure D).

Imagining two hundred billion stars is impossible. I once brought a two-pound box of salt to my astronomy class and dumped it all over the floor in spiral swaths, shaped vaguely like the spiral arms of the Milky Way. In this demonstration each individual grain of salt represents a star, with a possible system of satellites around it. Every single grain of salt is a star and the distance between adjacent grains is measured in trillions of miles. It is mindboggling to envision so much salt and think of each grain as a huge solar system. (And it was mindboggling to clean up all that salt when class was over.)

As we think of our sun as a member of a galaxy rather than the central member of our solar system, we have to find a new way to talk about distances. The nearest star to us, in our part of the Milky Way, has the exciting name Proxima Centauri and is over 25 trillion miles away. That distance is so great that light from that star takes over four years to reach us—longer than the political career of a one-term U.S. president. The stars on the other side of the galaxy are more than 300,000 trillion miles away, and it takes over 75,000 years for their light to reach us.[13]

The stars in a galaxy, like the satellites in a solar system, are bound together by gravity. Every one of the 200 billion stars in the Milky Way tugs on all the others. The closest stars are most strongly attracted, but all stars are attracted to each other. The same gravity that holds our solar system together also holds our galaxy together. The only difference is that the mass in the galaxy is not dominated by one central object in the center, like our sun, presiding like a rotund monarch over a retinue of commoners. In the galaxy the arrangement is more democratic, and we speak about the stars orbiting about the "center of mass" of the collection of stars as a whole, like children playing "ring around the rosy." Remarkably, gravity binds the entire galaxy in such a way that we can speak of the Milky Way as a single unit. We can then ask whether this gravitational unit interacts with other similar units—other galaxies. The answer, of course, is "of course."

Because the reach of gravity is infinite, the galaxies are themselves bound together into larger groups called clusters, which are so large it can take millions of years for light to pass from one end of a cluster to the other. The number of galaxies within a cluster can range from a handful to thousands.

Our Milky Way is part of a small cluster creatively labeled the "Local Group," with about fifty galaxies of various types. The Milky Way is at one end of the Local Group and the Andromeda galaxy is at the other. Visible as a faint smear on a dark, clear moonless night, Andromeda's light takes three million years to reach us. And beyond the scale of galactic clusters are the largest structures in the universe, known as superclusters. Just as stars are gathered into galaxies, and galaxies into clusters, so even the clusters are a part of a larger group. The larger superclusters have masses more than 10,000 trillion times that of our sun. They tend to be flattened into wall-like structures with big voids between them, like a pile of soap bubbles or a box full of blown-up balloons. Their size is impossible to envision. It takes more than 160 million years for light to get from one edge of our local supercluster to the other. And the large voids between the superclusters are more than twice that distance.

SO MUCH FOR SO LITTLE

Then Newton announced in due course
His own law of gravity's force:
"It goes, I declare,
As the inverted square
Of the distance from object to source!"

BRUCE ELLIOT

THE ORGANIZATIONAL POWERS of gravity are beyond belief, and we have just scratched the surface with our whirlwind tour through the cosmos. Right now, as you read these words, gravity holds you in your chair or on your couch. (I am assuming you are not an astronaut reading this book in outer space.) Gravity keeps your couch on the floor. You breathe air that gravity keeps securely wrapped around the earth. Outside your windows, gravity from the moon works the tides, moving them in and out—a cycling that does much to refresh the planet.

Gravity maintains the convection cycles that produce winds and rain. Hot air rises because it is lighter; cool air falls because it is heavier. The energy in the winds that cool us in the summer and bring rain in from the ocean comes from gravity. The energy of the hurricane and the tornado comes from gravity. The water that cascades over our hydroelectric dams is pulled by gravity.

The consistent temperature of the planet is possible only because gravity holds the earth in its orbit so faithfully, keeping it always about the same distance from the sun. The life-giving rays from the sun are produced because gravity compresses the atoms in the sun so they fuse together and give off energy. (We will look at this in more detail in chapter four.) Gravity empowers so many life-sustaining features of our world.

Life depends in less obvious ways on the structures that gravity has created in the universe. If small bits of matter were not gathered over billions of years into planets and stars, then debris from the heavens would rain down on us constantly. Sixty-five million years ago a great asteroid struck the earth with such violence that it left a crater in the Yucatan Peninsula in Mexico. The fallout from the asteroid, named Chicxulub, changed the atmosphere so dramatically that the dinosaurs were driven to extinction. If this were to happen today, the consequences for human life would be disastrous. And the only reason why it is unlikely to happen is that gravity has essentially vacuumed space so thoroughly that there just isn't much debris left to worry about. As it is, tens of thousands of meteorites are pulled by the earth's gravity into our atmosphere every year. But almost all of them burn up before they strike the earth (see insert figure E).

And beyond what is immediately relevant to us, gravity has created galaxies and clusters of galaxies that orbit about in an orderly fashion, making the universe predictable and stable.

The structures made possible by gravity are unimaginably complex. Planets, with many moons, orbiting stars; billions of stars orbiting in unison about galactic centers; collections of galaxies gathered together into clusters; great clusters arrayed in patterns that stretch partway across the entire universe. As a cosmic machine, the universe is grand and complex—a symphony conducted by gravity.

Not that long ago the heavens seemed an impenetrable mystery—unknown objects following unknown laws along paths that didn't quite make sense. The clouds began to lift when Galileo pointed his telescope at the heavens and made some simple observations. The moon, he noted, looked like the earth—just a big rock in the heavens held up by something he couldn't quite figure out. And not made out of some special heavenly material. Jupiter had moons orbiting it, following regular patterns. Apparently not everything orbits the earth. These simple observations inaugurated telescopic astronomy. Ever since, curious astronomers, from amateurs with binoculars to the operators of high-powered satellite dish arrays, have been peering into the heavens, getting a better handle on what is out there.

The twentieth century has witnessed the large-scale three-dimensional mapping of the universe. Just as European explorers traversed the globe in the fifteenth, sixteenth and seventeenth centuries and created our modern maps of the earth, so twentieth-century astronomers have, with telescopes rather than ships, traversed the universe and created our modern maps of the cosmos. The quest to map the universe continues to inspire bright young people, like my student Stephanie Capen, who we met in the introduction. The nearest such star is trillions of miles away, and it is surely remarkable to say with confidence that we know there are planets around stars at such distances.

Telescopes have revealed the great complexity of the universe. This is true whether they are Galileo's simple "optical tubes" or the high-tech machines used in investigations that locate tiny planets trillions of miles away. But this understanding does not simply fall from heaven, so to speak, just because we look at it. What we see through our telescopes are mute portraits offering no suggestions for how they should be understood—like old photos of people we don't recognize. The understanding we seek requires careful thinking and the development of theories to make sense of the observations. These theories are acts of great creativity that often require leaps of the imagination. The best theories—those that survive and become widely known—are the ones that suggest new observations. Careful reflection on the content of a theory sends the astronomer back to the telescope to look for something entirely new. Or, as has increasingly become the case, sends him or her to a colleague who knows how to run a modern telescope with a suggestion for a new place to look for something interesting.

Telescopes, of course, are but one of the many technologies that have extended the reach of our senses, letting us see things that are too dim, too small or have wavelengths too long or too short. Science as it has developed has extended all of our senses. But there is no greater scientific adventure than the one that has accompanied the telescope on its remarkable journey from Galileo's primitive spyglass, to the Hubble telescope orbiting the earth today, looking deep into the uncharted regions of space and back into cosmic history.

LEARNING TO
SEE THE UNIVERSE

Science Learns to Run

We are in the position of a little child entering a huge library filled with books in many different languages. The child knows someone must have written those books. It does not know how. It does not understand the languages in which they are written. The child dimly suspects a mysterious order in the arrangement of the books but doesn't know what it is. That, it seems to me, is the attitude of even the most intelligent human being toward God. We see a universe marvelously arranged and obeying certain laws, but only dimly understand these laws. Our limited minds cannot grasp the mysterious force that moves the constellations.

ALBERT EINSTEIN

THE DUTCHMAN HANS LIPPERSHEY invented the telescope in 1608. He owed his "aha" moment, at least according to legend, to children playing with lenses in his shop, where he made spectacles. The children were playing with pieces of the glass that Lippershey so painstakingly and precisely ground into lenses for his visually impaired customers. The children noticed that a weather vane on a nearby church looked larger when viewed through a pair of lenses.

Intrigued by the children's discovery, Lippershey installed lenses in a tube and invented what he called a "looker." Shortly after, he applied for a patent for his looker.

The patent office turned down his application on the grounds that the device was so simple that its workings could hardly remain secret. They were right. After all, it had been discovered by children. A year later, the great Italian scientist Galileo Galilei heard a vague description of the device and built his own looker. His first feeble attempt

Figure 3.1. On August 21, 1609, Galileo showed off his supposedly original invention to Venetian political leaders, including the chief magistrate—called the "Doge"—Leonardo Donato. The demonstration took place in the bell tower of Saint Mark's cathedral, from which one could look in any direction. Galileo's impressive performance got him named professor to the University of Padua for which he accepted a generous one thousand florin pension a year. (Wikimedia Commons)

magnified objects by a mere factor of three. With some effort he improved the performance until the magnification was around nine times, and got rich in the process.

In late August 1609 Galileo, then a professor at the University of Padua in the Venetian Republic, led some senators up a tower in Venice so they could look out to sea with his new spyglass. The senators assumed he had invented the remarkable device and were suitably impressed. Galileo's "optical tube," as they called it, enabled them to "discover at a much greater distance than usual the hulls and sails of the enemy, so that for two hours or more we can detect him before he detects us."[1] As the "inventor" of the amazing instrument, Galileo got a big raise and tenure.

Personal gain, although of interest to Galileo, was not his primary interest in the telescope. He wanted a closer look at the heavens in the hopes of seeing something there that would prove that the earth was going around the sun and not vice versa. Galileo was convinced that evidence must be there, somewhere, to establish the motion of the earth, as the great Polish thinker, Nicolaus Copernicus, had proposed in his book, *On the Revolutions of the Heavenly Spheres*, published in 1543.

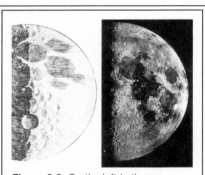

Figure 3.2. On the left is the moon, as seen through Galileo's telescope in 1609. Galileo's drawing was published in "Sidereus Nuncius" (Starry Messenger) in 1610. On the right is a modern photographic image of the same view. Galileo's observations revealed that the surface of the moon was irregular, with mountains and ridges like the earth. This was a controversial claim, although hard to refute. For two thousand years Western Europeans had accepted Aristotle's claim that the bodies in the heavens were perfect, smooth spheres. (ECeDee/Wikimedia Commons)

The new sun-centered model of the solar system had captured the imagination of some leading astronomers attracted to its simplicity. For decades, however, fans of the new model had been looking for *some* observational evidence that the earth was moving. But none had been discovered, which was puzzling. It seemed incomprehensible that the earth could be hurtling through space at seventy thousand miles per hour without some evidence that it was doing so.

Galileo, like any first-time user of a telescope, looked first at the moon. He was startled to find it "rough and uneven" with "huge prominences, deep valleys and chasms."[2] This ran counter to the prevailing view that bodies in the heavens were all perfectly spherical and composed of some perfect ethereal material not present on earth. The moon, Galileo would report, contradicting a two-thousand-year-old tradition going back to Aristotle, was clearly not "robed in a smooth and polished surface."[3] It looked much like the earth, in fact, undermining the standard view that the heavens were profoundly different than the earth, which was located at the center of the universe.

Galileo's innocent observation was quite radical in the first decade of the seventeenth century. The prevailing astronomical tradition had long taught that the heavens were perfect and unchanging, in contrast to the earth, which seemed in constant upheaval. This claim derived from the simple observation that change was almost never observed in the heavens. Christian theology, inspired by this pagan Greek idea, had interpreted the consistency of the night sky in terms of sin and the fall. Adam's sin had corrupted the earth but not the heavens, so the heavens—including the pattern of stars—were still in the same perfect state that God had originally created. Hell, being at the center of the earth, was also in the center of the universe, the worst spot in God's creation, of course, and as far away from the heavens as one could get. As one moved outward from the God-forsaken chaos at the center, things improved. The orbit of the moon was the boundary between the earthly and heavenly realm. The moon was in the heavens, beyond the sinister reach of the curse God had inaugurated in response to Adam's sin (see insert figure F). And yet it was not perfectly spherical. Why did it look so much like the earth if it was a *heavenly* body?

Early in January 1610, four wandering "stars" entered the field of view of Galileo's telescope, each of them always close to Jupiter. Galileo grew excited as he came to realize these wandering stars were moons orbiting Jupiter, proving that not everything revolved around the earth. This undermined the notion that the earth was somehow the central—although most corrupted—point of the creation. Europe's other great astronomer, Johannes Kepler, was thrilled with the discovery and went so far as to say, "Our Moon exists for us on the Earth, not for the other globes. Those four little moons exist for Jupiter, not for us. . . . From this line of reason we deduce with the highest degree of probability that Jupiter is inhabited."[4]

Galileo also found a way to look at the sun and located odd dark spots on it that came and went. Like the moon, the sun had a distinctly nonheavenly complexion. None of these discoveries provided the whiz-bang proof that the earth was in motion, but they certainly undermined other prevailing views. His more traditional contemporaries, however, were skeptical. Telescopes were rare, so most people couldn't check for themselves. And those who had telescopes found them so hard to oper-ate that they couldn't always see what Galileo claimed he saw. Gradu-ally, though, skepticism gave way to grudging respect as Galileo's dis-coveries—which he lorded over his peers as evidence of his superior intellect—were confirmed by others.

Galileo's star rose steadily in the firmament of Italian science as his discoveries became widely known. In less than two decades, however, his rising star would sputter and plummet back to earth in his cele-brated confrontation with the Roman Catholic Church.

In the last days of 1612 Galileo recorded in his notebook a "fixed star" that he observed near Jupiter. (The star was much farther away, of course, but it was next to Jupiter visually, like the moons.) Five days later he noted another new star near Jupiter. On January 28, 1613, he again noted two stars near Jupiter. The first one was just another star, now noted in star catalogs with the exciting name SAO 119234. The second one would prove more interesting, although it would take 250 years to realize just *how* interesting when it turned out to be the planet now named Neptune.

WOBBLES

I do not feel obligated to believe that the same God who has endowed us with sense, reason, and intellect has intended us to forgo their use.

GALILEO

IN 1633 AN elderly Galileo found himself kneeling before the Inqui-sition and recanting his long-held belief that the earth moves about the sun. Despite his best intentions—and many promises to his colleagues and critics—his telescope had failed to turn up compelling evidence for the radical idea that the earth moves. Contrary to widespread perception that the church was closed-minded and resistant to scientific ideas, the truth is that Galileo simply did not have *any* solid observational evidence. And based on both common sense and the best scientific understanding of the day, a moving earth should produce *some* noticeable effects. Many of Galileo's contemporaries—themselves astronomers and mathematicians—considered Copernicus's idea of a moving earth to be ridiculous for reasons that had nothing to do with the Bible or theology. And many of them agreed with Galileo about the motion of the earth, but believed the idea needed further development before it could be presented with any hope of being accepted. Galileo was far from the only Copernican of his generation, but he was the only one campaigning to change everybody's mind.

In 1597 Galileo received a copy of Johannes Kepler's book *The Cosmic Mystery,* which argued in favor of the sun-centered universe. Kepler was in many ways Galileo's Protestant counterpart and his only real peer in the pantheon of European astronomers. Galileo responded cordially to this first overture from Kepler, expressing his appreciation for a new "associate in the study of Truth who is a friend of Truth."

He went on to explain how he had been arguing quietly in favor of Copernicus for years and had "written many arguments in support of him and in refutation of the opposite view." But he feared ridicule and had not "dared to bring into the public light, frightened by the fate of Copernicus himself, our teacher who, though he acquired immortal fame with some, is yet to remain to an infinite number of others (for such is the number of fools) an object of ridicule and derision."[5] The word *fools,* unfortunately, was often on Galileo's lips as he enthusiastically ridiculed those who disagreed with him.

Galileo's advocacy for Copernicanism grew with each passing year, despite his consistent failure to find the evidence he promised. He became bolder and more aggressive. His fame spread across the continent and he grew steadily richer, with increasingly more lucrative academic postings and endless sales of telescopes. Gifted at debate and self-promotion, he steadily climbed the Italian social ladder, to the envy of his colleagues. He made enemies and backed many of his critics into

Figures 3.3-5. Galileo's celebrated trial before the Inquisition has acquired a mythical status in our culture. Paintings such as *Galileo Facing the Roman Inquisition* by Cristiano Banti (1857), plays like Bertolt Brecht's *Galileo* (1940), and even public television's documentary *Galileo's Battle for the Heavens* (2002) have portrayed Galileo as a great hero standing up to a backward and superstitious church. Urban legends report that Galileo was imprisoned and tortured, neither of which is true. Scholars who have examined the Galileo case argue that these portrayals are oversimplified. He was not tortured; the closest he came to imprisonment was house arrest in a luxury apartment; and there is ample evidence that the Italian political scene, over against the church, played a major role in his condemnation. (Cristiano Banti/Wikimedia Commons)

corners from where they could do nothing but seethe and look for an opportunity to get even. Some more cool-headed Jesuit astronomers were quietly teaching Copernican astronomy in Catholic universities, and, had Galileo not turned the motion of the earth into a political controversy, their diplomatic approach would have probably carried the day and avoided what became a great humiliation to the church. As it was, they were quite frustrated that Galileo's bombastic personal style got Copernicanism declared heretical and his book listed on an Index of Prohibited Books that good Catholics were not supposed to read.

The motion of the earth that we accept without a second thought today was troubling and without much support—scientific or otherwise—in the seventeenth century. It flew solidly in the face of a two-thousand-year tradition; there wasn't a single piece of observational data establishing it as true; it removed the earth from the center, where Christian theology thought it belonged, albeit in abject humiliation. Nevertheless, despite all these challenges, many Christians were slowly coming around to the new astronomy, and had Galileo been more diplomatic there would not have been any need for his great and celebrated confrontation between science and religion.

After recanting his heresies in 1633, Galileo spent the rest of his life in a comfortable apartment in Florence, under house arrest and forbidden to explore any longer the idea that the earth goes around the sun. He died in 1642.

THE BOYS ON THE SHORE

I do not know what I may appear to the world, but to myself I seem to have been only like a boy playing on the sea-shore, and diverting myself in now and then finding a smoother pebble or a prettier shell than ordinary, whilst the great ocean of truth lay all undiscovered before me.

ISAAC NEWTON

ON CHRISTMAS DAY in the year of Galileo's death, Isaac Newton was born on a farm in Woolsethorpe, England. His father, an illiterate farmer, had died a few months earlier and baby Isaac, premature and sickly, was not expected to live. He spent his first weeks in a shoebox behind the woodstove in the kitchen, but gradually became robust and healthy. A couple years later, alone and with a farm to run, his widowed mother married the stern and humorless Reverend Barnabas Smith, who didn't want any stepchildren. Little Isaac was turned over to his grandparents, who also didn't want him. At age twenty Isaac recalled his youthful sins in a notebook, one of which was "threatening my father and mother Smith to burne them and the house over them."[6]

Whatever the tragic childhood may have done to his spirit, Newton's remarkable mind emerged unscathed. Some have suggested that the isolation brought on by his mother's rejection increased Newton's intellectual powers, just as a blind person often has enhanced auditory skills. Whatever the influences, Newton prodigious intellect, recognized early by his teachers, who did a heroic job educating him, moved him slowly but steadily up the slopes of Mount Olympus until he took his place among its mythical residents.

Stephen Hawking, writing decades after Darwin and Einstein, calls Newton "a colossus without parallel in the history of science."[7] Newton single-handedly developed the remarkable theory of universal gravity that we looked at in chapter two—a theory that came to be viewed as omnicompetent and capable of explaining all the motions of the heavenly bodies. And it almost did. Almost.

Newton's theory provided a perfect explanation of the paths of just about everything in sight—the moon, the planets, the satellites around Jupiter and Saturn, and the occasional comets. Even cannonballs, arrows and marbles followed Newton's laws. And the earth no longer took its marching orders from Aristotle and Ptolemy, sailing merrily through space along a perfect elliptical path.

There was a tiny problem with the orbit of Uranus though, and in the resolution of that tiny problem we can catch a glimpse of how science works in practice.

Sir William Herschel officially discovered Uranus and nobody could have been more deserving of the recognition that followed. An accomplished musician and organist at the exclusive Octagon Chapel in Bath, England, Hershel was obsessed with telescopes and advanced the technology considerably, when he wasn't planning musical events. His telescopes became so famous that King George III gave him an annual stipend in exchange for relocating to Windsor so he could come by and see the telescopes at his convenience. Hershel's telescopes attracted countless visitors, including the king, who became something of a pest.

On one occasion the king dropped by the Herschels' home with the elderly archbishop of Canterbury in tow to show him the latest telescope, a forty-foot masterpiece and the only one of its kind. "Come, my lord bishop," said the king, "I will show you the way to heaven."

Hershel discovered Uranus in 1781 while he was living in Bath, just thirty-three years after John Wesley had started the Kingswood school there. The planet, which he immediately named Georgius Sidum (George's Star) after George III, is visible to the naked eye and had been observed many times before Herschel officially "discovered" it to be something other than just one more star to put in the catalog. (Telescopes were steadily improving and finding so many new stars that the discoveries were now ho-hum affairs.) He announced the new star in March 1781, after sweeping the night sky several times with his telescope. "George's Star" was so far away—almost two billion miles— that its discovery doubled the known size of the solar system. Astronomers outside England were—understandably perhaps—dismayed at the prospects of a planet named George, and it wasn't long until they had settled on its present name.

Figure 3.6. William Hershel's forty-foot telescope as it looked in 1789. It was the grandest telescope in the world at the time and demanded enormous dedication and patronage to construct and operate. (Wikimedia Commons)

Once Uranus joined the planetary family, its orbit was carefully plotted as yet another check of Newton's now famous and widely accepted law of gravity. Did Newton's law of universal gravity reach all the way out to this new part of the solar system? Unfortunately

the answer seemed to be no. Newtonians were unsettled. Uranus did
not travel in the elliptical path specified by Newton's theory. It occasionally veered off course, as though it had a bit of a wobble, like a bi-
cycle with a bent wheel or a runner with a rock in her shoe. Up to this
point Newton's theory had been applied only to bodies within the solar
system. The most distant body from the sun had been Saturn, which
was much closer than Uranus. Some astronomers speculated that Newton's theory of gravity wasn't universal—the gravity from the sun would
not faithfully follow Newton's laws at arbitrarily large distances. After
all, two billion miles is far. Can we really expect the sun to tug on
something so far away and keep it moving in a nice smooth orbit, like
the planets that are closer?

True believers said yes, even in the face of evidence to the contrary.
After all, Newton's gravitational equation worked like a charm for the
moon and several other planets. It worked so well its enthusiasts were
referring to God as a great mathematician and concluding that Newton
had discovered his formulas. Why wouldn't God's mathematics work
for Uranus? Surely the grand system that God ordained for the rest of
the planets would work for this new member of the planetary family.
But, in defiance of such enthusiasm, Uranus continued to wobble off its
elliptical course with infuriating indifference to Newton's theory.

The French astronomer Urbain Le Verrier was one of Newton's true
believers. Convinced that Newton's theory must work everywhere, he
set out to solve the problem of Uranus's wobble. He intuited that there
must be another planet beyond Uranus that occasionally got close
enough to disturb its perfect elliptical orbit about the sun. For months
Le Verrier worked on mathematical equations calculating where a new
planet would have to be to explain the wobble of Uranus. He filled page
after page with calculations. It was a dreadfully messy problem.

Le Verrier started with the observations of Uranus's location in the
night sky, which were always just a celestial longitude and latitude—so
many degrees above the horizon, and so many degrees east or west.
Such observations contained no information about the distance to the
wobbling planet. He then adjusted for the position of the earth, which
was constantly moving, to figure out where Uranus actually was, rather

than where it appeared to be. Such observations, after much work, yielded up the actual path of the planet, essentially establishing what it would look like if he had a God's-eye view from above the solar system—the sort of picture commonly presented in textbooks.

The actual path of Uranus differed ever so *slightly*, and only *occasionally*, from the path predicted by Newton's equations. Would this discrepancy go away if there were another planet beyond Uranus? Such a planet would move about the sun more slowly than Uranus, which takes eighty-four years for a complete cycle. It would influence Uranus only slightly, except on those rare occasions when they were close together, like two very different runners on a single track that interact only when one passes the other.

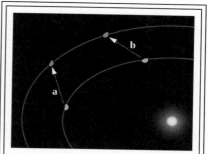

Figure 3.7. This illustration shows two planets moving clockwise around the sun and interacting gravitationally, as Uranus and Neptune do occasionally. The outer planet takes more time to travel around the sun, so the inner planet occasionally overtakes it. At position "a," the outer planet pulls on the inner one and makes it go faster. At "b," the reverse is true and the inner planet slows down. This perturbing influence is what led to the discovery of the planet Neptune.

Le Verrier calculated where the hypothetical planet would need to be, an act of great faith in the reliability of Newton's equations. Now he needed a skilled observer with a sophisticated telescope to find this location in the sky and see if there was anything there. Unable to inspire his fellow French astronomers to search, he sent his results to an observatory in Germany. On the night of September 23, 1846, just hours after getting a letter from Le Verrier, a Berlin astronomer sat down to decipher the newly arrived calculations. He pointed his telescope at the spot in the sky where Le Verrier's calculations said a hypothetical planet was supposed to be located and, sure enough, found the planet we now call Neptune, just after midnight on September 24. The search took him only one hour, because he knew where to look.

Le Verrier had used mathematics not to describe things that were already known but to discover something entirely new about the universe. One of his fellow scientists, who lobbied to name the planet after him, said Le Verrier had discovered a planet with "the point of his pen."[8] It was a stunning confirmation of Newton's theory of gravity, further increasing the already considerable confidence people had in the theory. Newton's original intuition, which seems almost reckless in retrospect, was that a rational God would create a world with consistent laws that did not vary as one moved from one place to the next. He was right.

WHAT YOU SEE IS NOT WHAT YOU GET

Seeing is an experience. A retinal reaction is only a physical state. . . .
People, not their eyes, see. Cameras, and eye-balls, are blind . . .
there is more to seeing than meets the eyeball.

NORWOOD RUSSELL HANSON

THE DISCOVERY OF Neptune opens a window into the nature of science. For starters, it illustrates the deep relationship between theories and observations—the "two legs" I talked about in chapter two. In this case, the two legs moving science forward were actually two different people—a mathematician who knew how numbers worked and an astronomer who knew how telescopes worked. This division of labor persists today. The discovery also reveals a deeply counterintuitive lesson about the relationship between theories and experiments, and what should be done when they disagree. The discovery of Neptune reveals the wisdom of trusting an established theory, even when observations contradict it. There is a supposed rule in science that observations always triumph over theories, when they disagree, but the reality—and actual practice—suggests otherwise. A solid theory can withstand the assault of a few troubling observations, as long as there is hope that there might be some way to handle the trouble. This explains why scientists pay little heed when a wide-ranging and well-established theory is assaulted by critics armed with a small number of facts. The discovery of Neptune also shows how theories are necessary to even understand facts. Once the new planet officially existed, astronomers learned that it had been observed several times before, most notably by Galileo, with his newly minted telescope, in December 1612 and January 1613. Galileo thought the dim point of light was a star, not a planet. Once again we see the interesting relation between theory and observation. In this case, the theory was necessary to properly interpret the observation. This happens often in science.

In 1859, history appeared to be repeating itself. Le Verrier reported an irregularity in the orbit of Mercury. Like Uranus, Mercury was not following the path predicted by Newton's theory of gravity and was mis-behaving in a much more inter-esting way. According to New-ton's theory, bodies moving under the influence of gravity follow el-liptical paths that repeat. Some, like the earth, move in ellipses that are almost perfect circles. Others, like Halley's comet, move in long skinny orbits shaped like hot dogs. Of course, the planets all move in orbits closer to circles than hot dogs, but both shapes are variations on the elliptical theme.

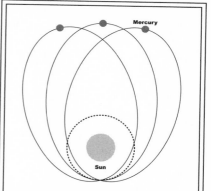

Figure 3.8. Contrary to Newton's theory of gravity, the orbit of Mercury does not retrace the same path each time. Instead, the long axis of the orbit moves by a fixed amount each time the planet goes around the sun. (This image is exaggerated so you can see the effect. Mercury's actual orbit is much closer to being a perfect circle, and the change in the orbit each time around is much smaller than pictured here.)

Whatever the actual shape of the ellipse though, the path should be *stable*. The planet should stay on track, so to speak, repeating the same path. Mercury did not do this. Its orbit was slightly different each trip around the sun, but in an elegant and highly regular way resembling the patterns that can be created with the Spiro-graph children's toy (see fig. 3.8). The "regular irregularity" was known as the *precession* of Mercury's orbit.

Le Verrier tried to explain the interesting pattern—the precession—of Mercury was the effects from the other nearby planets, Venus and Earth. No luck. So, inspired by his success with Neptune, he made another bold prediction that Mercury's wobble was caused by its gravitational interactions with another planet, this one invisible against the glare of the sun. The hypothetical planet was called Vulcan, later to become famous as the name of the home planet of Star Trek's beloved alien, Mr. Spock. Alas, Vulcan was never discovered and history did not repeat itself.

BEYOND NEWTON

On my planet "to rest" is to rest, to cease using energy.
To me it is quite illogical to run up and down on
green grass using energy instead of saving it.

MR. SPOCK IN *SHORE LEAVE*

THE PROBLEM OF Mercury remained a mystery into the twentieth century and was ultimately resolved through a happy accident involving a revolutionary new theory about gravity developed by Albert Einstein. To appreciate the significance of this we have to look more closely at what Newton's theory did and did not explain. In so doing we get additional insight into the way that science advances by returning to unsolved mysteries.

Newton's explanation of gravity worked so well that people overlooked its failure to actually explain what gravity was. In time they forgot that this was even a legitimate scientific question. The mystery of gravity simply drifted off the island of science to perhaps wash up on the shores of metaphysics or theology.

Scientists in Newton's time, however, were mystified by gravity. What exactly was this strange force that could reach out through empty space? What were these invisible bands that joined the earth to the sun, the moon to the earth, and people to the ground? Some skeptics thought Newton's theory was nonsense—a seventeenth-century version of spoon bending or mind reading. Critics called the suggestion that bodies could interact across empty space "occultic." The French philosopher René Descartes developed an entirely different explanation for the motions of the planets to get around the strange idea of "action at a distance." In Descartes's scheme space was filled with fluid that moved around in a vortex like a whirlpool. The planets were carried around in this vortex, like leaves floating in a whirlpool, orbiting about the drain. This removed the need to believe in any spooky action at a distance.

Newton, his contemporaries, and eventually even the reluctant French rejected Descartes's theory of vortices. But this was not because Newton explained how gravity worked. Far from it. His rather unsatisfactory position was that he would "frame no hypotheses" about gravity other than to claim, quite successfully, that his equations *described* it correctly. This would be analogous to a child "understanding" that hitting the switch makes the light come on, while knowing absolutely nothing about electricity.

Newton's theory of gravity was so successful in describing gravitational interactions that scientists paid little attention to the fact that the theory was silent on the nature of the strange force that bodies seemed to exert on each other. In this history we get a backdoor insight into the success of science—by simply ignoring a deep question, science creates the impression that it can solve any problem. Deep questions are always knocking on the door of science, asking to be invited inside. By judicious selection of what gets through the door, science purchases its great success at explaining "everything."

Progress on understanding the nature of gravity would wait until the twentieth century, when Albert Einstein opened the door and invited this deep question inside.

Einstein exploded onto the scientific scene in 1905, publishing several groundbreaking papers that began to reshape our ideas about the nature of space and time. At the time he was a lowly clerk in a patent office in Switzerland, hardly a posting from which one might expect to topple the great Isaac Newton. But this is exactly what happened.

Einstein's new theory of gravity was called "general relativity." The densely mathematical theory treated gravity very differently than Newton had done. In Einstein's theory, bodies in space do not reach out across empty space and exert forces on each other. Rather, space is treated as a real medium—picture a thin fog spread throughout the universe—and bodies in this space distort and twist it with their mass.

Figures 3.9-10. Isaac Newton (left, 1642-1727) and Albert Einstein (1879-1955) provided two very different explanations for gravity. Newton's theory, ambitiously labeled a theory of "universal gravity," turned out to be a very good approximation that worked well for weak gravitational fields, and objects moving at reasonable speeds. (Newton: Used by permission. ©Georgios Kollidas/depositphotos; Einstein: Ferdinand Schmutzer/Wikimedia Commons)

The sun, for example, being very massive, greatly distorts the space around it, like a sumo wrestler sitting on a trampoline or a finger pushing into a bowl of Jell-O. The planets around the sun travel through this distorted space, which makes them follow elliptical paths, sort of like a tennis ball might roll on the trampoline around the sumo wrestler.

The distortion of space caused by bodies like the sun is greatest near the sun, of course, which is where Einstein proposed to conduct a really ingenious observational test of his theory. Away from the sun, Einstein's theory and Newton's theory made similar predictions about the behavior of moving bodies. But near the sun, Einstein's theory said that the space would be so distorted that even a beam of light passing through it would be deflected, like a baseball pitcher's curve ball.

The problem, of course, is that any beam of light—such as might come from a star—passing near the sun would be completely overwhelmed by the light from the sun. The stars, for example, are simply not visible during the day because the sun's brightness overwhelms them. But there is one time when the stars join the sun in the sky—during an eclipse. Einstein calculated how much deflection a beam of starlight would experience if it passed very close to the sun. He made a detailed prediction that could be tested by observations that could be made during an eclipse, which is the only time the stars can be seen when the sun is overhead—assuming clouds are not in the way.

Testing Einstein's new theory of gravity was a major scientific event. If general relativity passed the observational tests, it would replace Newton's theory, something that most people thought would never occur. Newton's venerable prestige and unfathomable intellect had been towering over science for more than two centuries. Biographers had stripped Newton of all his pedestrian finitude and turned him into a mythic symbol of genius. If anyone had spoken directly to God about how the world had been created, it was Isaac Newton. "Nearer the gods no mortal may approach," wrote Edmund Halley in a preface to an edition of Newton's *Principia Mathematica*.

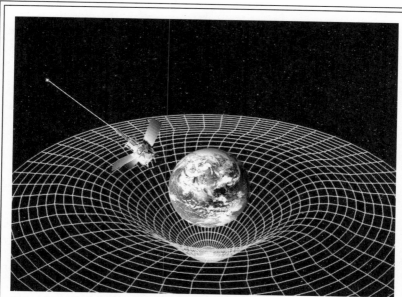

Figure 3.11. Einstein explained gravity as a distortion of the space around a body, rather than the attraction of bodies for each other. Here we see a satellite orbiting the earth, traveling through space that has been distorted by the earth. (NASA)

Einstein was only too aware that displacing Newton was like telling all the children in the world there is no Santa Claus. In an elegant acknowledgment he wrote: "Newton, forgive me. You found the only way which in your age was just barely possible for a man with the highest powers of thought and creativity. The concepts which you created are guiding our thinking in physics even today."[9]

THE WONDER OF
THE COSMOS

How the Universe Got a History

Not only is the universe stranger than we imagine,
it is stranger than we can imagine.

SIR ARTHUR EDDINGTON

Newton's theory of universal gravity, presented to the world in his now-famous book the *Principia*, guided physics and inspired all of science for more than two centuries. It became the gold standard for knowledge, emulated by those seeking to illuminate the dark corners of human understanding. Everyone, from political theorists like John Locke and economists like Adam Smith, looked to it as a model for organizing knowledge in their own fields of interests. John Wesley listed the *Principia* in the curriculum of the second-year students at Kingswood.[1]

Newton's gold-plated theory of gravity was laid to rest in 1919 by a split-second interaction of a beam of starlight with the gravity of the sun, destined to become the single most important scientific observation ever made. The celebrity starlight began its long journey from the Hyades star cluster to earth more than two centuries ago, at roughly the time that Captain Cook and his crew headed off on their legendary voyage to Tahiti. In the middle of the morning of May 29, 1919, the light entered our solar system en route to earth, traversing the orbits of the eight planets one by one. (Pluto had not yet begun its short-lived residence on the planetary roster.) Scheduled to hit the earth at midday, the light would normally be invisible against the glare of the sun, but this day was hosting an eclipse, so the stars in the Hyades cluster should be visible while the moon was blocking the sun.[2]

The British astronomer and Quaker Sir Arthur Eddington had traveled to the island of Principe, off the coast of West Africa, to observe the eclipse in all its fullness. He had equipment and a team in place to record the stellar event. Eddington had convinced the Royal Society, which once claimed Isaac Newton as its president, to fund the expensive project. May 29 dawned cloudy. The team on Principe fretted under torrential downpours, staring hopefully at the heavens and muttering encouragements to each other. The eclipse began under cloud cover, and above the heads of some very discouraged British astronomers. But at the last moment, as if God was authoring the revelation, the clouds broke, an eclipsed sun appeared, and Eddington feverishly began to slide glass photographic plates in and out of his camera, recording the position of the Hyades.

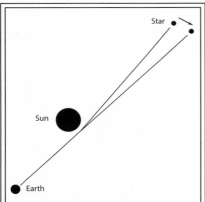

Figure 4.1. When starlight is deflected from its normally straight path, the star will appear to be in a different location. Here we see how the star appears to be to the right of its normal location.

Eight minutes prior to being captured by Eddington's camera, the light that left the Hyades cluster in 1768 grazed the edge of the sun, passing through our solar system's strongest gravitational region. The sun's intense gravity altered the path of the light and, sure enough, the light curved just as Einstein predicted it would.

When the eclipse and its Kodak moment had passed, Eddington began to make measurements on his photographic plates. The starlight had been bent just as Einstein predicted. The Hyades' apparent home in the heavens was displaced ever so slightly. Eddington looked up from his plates at a vastly different world. Isaac Newton's theory of universal gravity, like the sun in the photos on his plates, had just been eclipsed.

Albert Einstein, the respected but not-yet-iconic originator of the strange theory that predicted the deflection of the starlight, so the story goes, slept peacefully while Eddington made his observations. In contrast, Max Planck, the editor of the *Annalen der Physik*, which would publish Eddington's result, remained awake, eagerly anticipating a cable from Principe. Einstein would later quip—tongue comfortably lodged in cheek—that Planck need not have lost any sleep, for the theory being tested was so beautiful that it could not possibly fail to be confirmed by Eddington's measurements. Eddington later commented, "I think there should be a law of Nature to prevent a star from behaving in this absurd way!"[3]

The confirmation of general relativity in 1919 is one of those mythmaking moments in history—like Galileo's trial before the Inquisition in 1633 or Huxley's confrontation with Wilberforce over evolution in 1860—when long-burning fuses reach their destination and things explode.

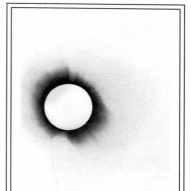

Figure 4.2. This is the negative of the 1919 solar eclipse taken from the report of Sir Arthur Eddington on the expedition to verify Einstein's prediction of the bending of light around the sun. (F. W. Dyson, A. S. Eddington and C. Davidson, "A Determination of the Deflection of Light by the Sun's Gravitational Field, from Observations Made at the Total Eclipse of May 29, 1919," *Philosophical Transactions of the Royal Society*, vol. 220 [January 1, 1920]: 332 <http://rsta.royal societypublishing.org/content /220/571-581/291.full.pdf+html>.)

THE UNIVERSE GETS A HISTORY

The modern world began on 29 May 1919 when photographs of a solar eclipse, taken on the island of Principe off West Africa and at Sobral in Brazil, confirmed the truth of a new theory of the universe.

PAUL JOHNSON

THE END OF the Newtonian era—what we now call *classical physics*—
marked an extraordinary change in our perception of ourselves and our
world. One historian has said that replacement of Newton's theory of
gravity inaugurated the modern world. There is, of course, far more to the
modern world than simply a new theory of gravity, but this symbolic top-
pling of Newton was as good a starting point as any. The modern world
disclosed by new theories like relativity was quite different from the more
commonsense world of classical physics. Eddington's measurements established that the Hyades cluster was somewhere other than where it appeared. We can look over *here* for it and actually find it. But somehow it
was, said Einstein, over *there*, in a different place. And, of course, those
who had put their trust in the traditional Newtonian picture of the world
turned out to be deceived. "Beware received wisdom" was the emerging
refrain as new science overturned traditional understandings.

The London papers reported Eddington's discovery with two-inch
headlines and preposterous hyperbole, declaring "Lights All Askew in
the Heavens." A more accurate headline would have read "A Few Lights
Moved by a Tiny Amount." The seer who had predicted this was a
forty-year-old Jewish physicist who had just moved from academia to
the center of Western culture, where he would take up residence as a
brooding, detached and haunting presence, a presence only marginally
diminished by his death in 1955.

GOODBYE PLANET VULCAN

Creating a new theory is not like destroying an old barn and erecting a
skyscraper in its place. It is rather like climbing a mountain, gaining new and
wider views, discovering unexpected connections between our starting point
and its rich environment. But the point from which we started out still exists
and can be seen, although it appears smaller and forms a tiny part of our broad
view gained by the mastery of the obstacles on our adventurous way up.

ALBERT EINSTEIN

ONCE AGAIN, WE see both the power of the scientific approach as
well as the complex and idiosyncratic relationship between theory and

observation. In the case of Newton's theory, the contradictory observations of both Uranus and Mercury were perceived as problems to be solved *within* the theory, not challenges to the theory itself. The stunning success in finding Neptune, of course, did much to validate Newton's theory. But the ongoing failure to explain the irregularities in the orbit of Mercury was tolerated as little more than a puzzle to be solved.

Both of these responses provide insights into the deeply personal character of science and illustrate the important role played by informed judgment. The success of Newton's theory of gravity was impressive. Precise mathematical calculations were repeatedly applied to bodies in space and the match between theory and observation for the moon, Mars, Jupiter and so on was simply too good not to be true. A level of trust and confidence was built up in the theory until people were willing to give the theory the benefit of the doubt, even as small anomalies appeared. By analogy, you might have a close friend whose loyalty has been validated many times over the years. If someone reports a betrayal to you, you would most likely be skeptical, believing the communication to be wrong or misunderstood. Years of trust are not readily destroyed by a single counterexample. And if trust in the face of contradictory evidence is *rewarded*—as it was with the discovery of Neptune—that trust becomes even deeper. Trust in Newton's theory of gravity was such that even a century of failure to explain the orbit of Mercury could not undermine it.

Eddington's eclipse observations provide a rather different insight into the nature of science. In this case a single, relatively modest observation dramatically confirmed a new explanation for gravity, sweeping Newton aside in the process. The stars in the Hyades cluster were moved by the tiniest amount, far less than the irregularity associated with the orbit of Mercury. And general relativity had no century-long track record of impressive explanations. The theory didn't even exist when Einstein was in college and had no stunning observational successes prior to the eclipse measurements. So how did general relativity fare so well?

Several factors contributed to the success of general relativity. In the two decades prior to Eddington's measurements, Newton's ideas—which were much broader than simply gravity—had been weighed in

LIGHTS ALL ASKEW IN THE HEAVENS

Men of Science More or Less Agog Over Results of Eclipse Observations.

EINSTEIN THEORY TRIUMPHS

Stars Not Where They Seemed or Were Calculated to be, but Nobody Need Worry.

A BOOK FOR 12 WISE MEN

No More in All the World Could Comprehend It, Said Einstein When His Daring Publishers Accepted It.

Special Cable to THE NEW YORK TIMES.
LONDON, Nov. 9.—Efforts made to put in words intelligible to the non-scientific public the Einstein theory of light proved by the eclipse expedition so far have not been very successful. The new theory was discussed at a recent meeting of the Royal Society and Royal Astronomical Society, Sir Joseph Thomson, President of the Royal Society, declares it is not possible to put Einstein's theory into really intelligible words, yet at the same time Thomson adds:

"The results of the eclipse expedition demonstrating that the rays of light from the stars are bent or deflected from their normal course by other aerial bodies acting upon them and consequently the inference that light has weight form a most important contribution to the laws of gravity given us since Newton laid down his principles."

Thompson states that the difference between theories of Newton and those of Einstein are infinitesimal in a popular sense, and as they are purely mathematical and can only be expressed in strictly scientific terms it is useless to endeavor to detail them for the man in the street.

"What is easily understandable," he continued, "is that Einstein predicted the deflection of the starlight when it passed the sun, and the recent eclipse has provided a demonstration of the correctness of the prediction.

"His second theory as to the anomalous motion of the planet Mercury has also been verified, but his third prediction, which dealt with certain sun lines, is still indefinite."

Asked if recent discoveries meant a reversal of the laws of gravity as defined by Newton, Sir Joseph said they highly mathematical problems the new conceptions of Einstein, whereby space became warped or curled under certain circumstances, would have to be taken into account.

Vastly different conceptions which are involved in this discovery and the necessity for taking Einstein's theory more into account were voiced by a member of the expedition, who pointed out that it meant, among other things, that two lines normally known as parallel do meet eventually, that a circle is not really circular, that three angles of a triangle do not necessarily make the sum total of two right angles.

"Enough has been said to show the importance of Einstein's theory, even if it cannot be expressed clearly in words," laughed this astronomer.

Dr. W. J. S. Lockyer, another astronomer, said:

"The discoveries, while very important, did not, however, affect anything on this earth. They do not personally concern ordinary human beings; only astronomers are affected. It has hitherto been understood that light traveled in a straight line. Now we find it travels in a curve. It therefore follows that any object, such as a star, is not necessarily in the direction in which it appears to be astronomically.

"This is very important, of course. For one thing, a star may be a considerable distance further away than we have hitherto counted it. This will not affect navigation, but it means corrections will have to be made."

One of the speakers at the Royal Society's meeting suggested that Euclid was knocked out. Schoolboys should not rejoice prematurely, for it is pointed out that Euclid laid down the axiom that parallel straight lines, if produced ever so far, would not meet. He said nothing about light lines.

Some cynics suggest that the Einstein theory is only a scientific version of the well-known phenomenon that a coin in a basin of water is not on the spot where it seems to be and what is new in the refraction of light.

Albert Einstein is a Swiss citizen, about 50 years of age. After occupying a position as Professor of Mathematical Physics at the Zurich Polytechnic School and afterward at Prague University, he was elected a member of Emperor William's Scientific Academy in Berlin at the outbreak of the war. Dr. Einstein protested against the German professors' manifesto approving of Germany's participation in the war, and at its conclusion he welcomed the revolution. He has been living in Berlin for about six years.

When he offered his last important work to the publishers he warned them there were not more than twelve persons in the whole world who would understand it, but the publishers took the risk.

The New York Times
Published: November 10, 1919
Copyright © The New York Times

Figure 4.3. The historic headline in the *New York Times*, and the associated story, presented a humorously misconstrued version of Eddington's classic observation. ("Lights All Askew in the Heavens," *The New York Times,* November 10, 1919.)

the balances several times and found wanting. The new quantum theory of the atom was very un-Newtonian, as were new ideas about space and time established in Einstein's theory of special relativity, a precursor to general relativity. So there were some reasons to be concerned about Newton's theory. But the main reason for the rapid ascendancy of the new theory has to do with the *strangeness* of the predictions Einstein made. The suggestion that the stars in the heavens will actually appear in a new location is truly strange. If such an odd and unbelievable prediction comes true, then surely the theory behind the prediction must also be true.

In this historical episode we see once again the role of *judgment* in science. A result is inspected within the context of countless other insights and is evaluated not in terms of simple rules but by collective wisdom. The great Hungarian philosopher of science Michael Polanyi

(1891-1976) emphasized that scientific knowledge is always personal—there is no such thing as knowledge that is simply "out there." All truth claims begin as *belief* and are made by people who are more than simply the sum total of the observations they have made. Facts reside in heads, not in nature.[4]

Quantum Theory

Anyone who is not shocked by quantum theory has not understood it.

NEILS BOHR

"Quantum theory contains some of the strangest ideas in all of science. Many physicists, including Einstein, could not accept it and it took a couple of generations of physicists until everyone became comfortable with it. The most puzzling part of the new theory was the realization that electrons were waves and not neat little "balls." In the atom, these waves wrap around the nucleus in such a way that the electron can be located only at certain specific spots but can never be between those spots. This would be like our solar system if there were some law that prevented a planet from being located between the orbits of Venus and Earth.

Prior to the discovery of quantum theory everybody thought that the atom was basically just a miniature solar system, with planetary electrons orbiting about a nuclear sun.

Quantum theory also introduced *uncertainty* into physics. The wave-like electron could never be located precisely. All we could do was specify probabilities of where it could be found. And the act of measuring its location would send it off to another location.

The odd phenomena associated with quantum theory revealed that the world of the very small was nothing like the larger world. Physics inside the atom bore little resemblance to physics on the scale of the solar system.

The confirmation of Einstein's theory put general relativity on the radar screens of physicists everywhere, and it wasn't long until even stranger new ideas began to emerge from the theory. In the background of all this was the happy discovery that Einstein's theory explained the irregularity in the orbit of Mercury. Close to the sun, where Mercury orbits, starlight curves, and no planet Vulcan hides, the distortion of space is so great that things don't behave in Newtonian ways. The puzzling but regular shifting of Mercury's orbit actually emerges as a *prediction* of general relativity. Sit down with the equations for a long afternoon of calculating orbits close to the sun and a precisely specified, non-Newtonian orbit that exactly matches Mercury's will appear on the page in front of you.

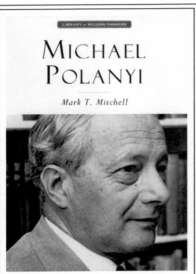

Figure 4.4. "We must recognize belief as the source of all knowledge. Tacit assent and intellectual passions, the shaping of an idiom and of a cultural heritage, affiliation to a likeminded community: such are the impulses which shape our vision of the nature of things on which we rely for our mastery of things. No intelligence, however critical or original, can operate outside such a fiduciary framework."—Michael Polanyi

Unlike the bending of starlight, however, the odd behavior of Mercury was well-known before general relativity. Predicting things that are already known does not have quite the same whiz-bang effect as predicting things that are not already known. Most thoughtful people are unimpressed, for example, when Bible code gurus find Kennedy's assassination "predicted" in the Bible. Far more impressive would be the prediction of a world leader's assassination *before* it happened. Technically we call such backward predictions *retrodictions*. General relativity we say *could* have predicted the motion of Mercury if it wasn't already known.

In any event, the orbit of Mercury stopped being mysterious, Newton's theory was demoted from being "universal" to being a good approximation that works well in *most* but not all settings. And a powerful new theory emerged—one that treated gravity as a distortion of space rather than a force between masses.

ON TO THE BIG BANG

But the years of anxious searching in the dark, with their intense longing,
their alternations of confidence and exhaustion, and the final emergence into
the light—only those who have experienced it can understand that.

ALBERT EINSTEIN

IN THE WAKE of Eddington's measurements during the eclipse, interest grew in the theory that explained the odd result. Remarkably, with some approximations, the theory could describe the entire universe, which attracted great interest on the part of the few who could understand it. Mathematical physicists heroically mastered the esoteric foundations of general relativity and began to contemplate the interesting solutions to its equations. One such solution suggested that the universe might be changing. Another suggested it was contracting. Einstein—still the referee of his own theory—rejected both possibilities because no observational evidence of any sort existed to imply that the universe was expanding. Einstein managed to find a fudge factor, however, to incorporate into the theory to do away with the strange suggestion that the universe was changing in size.

In 1929, using a massive telescope with a hundred-inch-wide mirror at Mount Wilson Observatory near Los Angeles, the astronomer Edwin Hubble discovered, to his surprise, that the universe was indeed expanding. Using new techniques to measure the distances to all the known galaxies, he discovered that the galaxies were all moving away from each other. Everywhere he looked in the universe the galaxies were separating. This could mean only that the universe was getting bigger. Einstein ruefully removed the fudge factor from his theory two years later, calling it the "greatest blunder of my career." The fudge factor was allowed in his theory as a sort of mathematical trick, but it was arbitrary and didn't belong, and he was quite relieved to remove it.

The expanding universe, while a mind-boggling concept, had to be taken seriously. The most natural version of Einstein's celebrated theory of gravity said that the universe had to be expanding or contracting. Absent a fudge factor, those were the only options. Hubble's observa-

Figure 4.5. This picture was taken in 1922 during the construction of the 100-inch telescope with which Hubble discovered the galactic red shifts, which implied that the universe was expanding. (c. 1918/www.astrosurf.com/re/100inch_mount_wilson_small.jpg)

tions confirmed the expansion option. But what did it mean to say the universe was *expanding*? The problem arises when we start to work our way backward in time. Running the universe in reverse means that the galaxies are all approaching each other and, if we run back far enough, all the galaxies are scrunched into a single large mass. Picture a hornet's nest that you smash with a stick. The hornets fly and out and gradually disperse. Now imagine what a video of the event would look like running in reverse—the hornets would all converge back into the hive. But what does it mean to say that all the galaxies—indeed everything—in the universe erupted out of some cosmic beehive at some point in the distant past?

The answer to this most puzzling of questions came from an unlikely source—a Belgian priest-astrophysicist named Georges Lemaître. A brilliant mathematician in priestly robes, the paradoxical Lemaître had fought the Germans in the trenches of WWI, where he observed the first use of chlorine gas, pointed out an error in the military ballistic manual and received an award for bravery.[5]

Lemaître earned his Ph.D. in mathematics, and an undergraduate degree in Catholic philosophy the year after Eddington's famous eclipse observation. Proceeding immediately to seminary, he was delighted to discover that his professors were very interested in relativity—not standard seminary fare. He was ordained in 1923.

Lemaître was hooked on relativity and the speculations arising out of it. He was especially intrigued by the idea that the universe should be expanding or contracting, something that contradicted centuries of observation until Hubble made his important observations of the galaxies. Lemaître boldly speculated—following the evidence where it leads—that an expanding universe could have originated only in some kind of primordial explosion. This explosion must have somehow involved the entire universe—whatever that could mean—giving rise to the expanding universe that Hubble had discovered.

Critics were put off by the robed cleric in their midst preaching unwanted "sermons" about the beginning of the universe. Some cried foul and accused Lemaître of smuggling a supernatural explanation into cosmology. Such a well-defined beginning to the universe sounded an awful lot like the first verse of Genesis: "In the beginning God created the heavens and the earth." And was it really a coincidence that professor Lemaître was also a *priest*?

Even the deeply religious Eddington was put off by Lemaître's suggestion that the world had a beginning: "We have

Figure 4.6. The great but unsung Belgian physicist George Lemaître (1894-1966), lecturing on general relativity in his priest's robe. He embodied a harmony of science and religion, to the puzzlement of some of his peers. (Wikimedia Commons)

come to an abrupt end of space-time—only we generally call it the "beginning" . . . philosophically the notion of a beginning of the present order of Nature is repugnant to me."[6]

Lemaître insisted that he was simply following the evidence where it led. And he consoled Eddington that the beginning he had in mind would precede the "present order of Nature." To this Eddington, now following the lead of a junior scientist who he had done much to educate a few years earlier, conceded inarticulately and ambiguously: "If this suggestion is correct, the beginning of the world happened a little before the beginning of space and time. I think that such a beginning of the world is far enough from the present order of Nature to be not repugnant at all."[7]

The nature of Lemaître's "beginning" plagued him for years. The idea was so foreign to science, and physics in particular, that few could take it seriously as science. And it was so suggestive of the traditional creation story that religious pundits could not resist connecting the dots and making it into a supernatural creation event, despite Lemaître's insistent protests to the contrary.

Lemaître even had a bit of a dust-up with Pope Pius XII in 1951, who had stated publically that Lemaître's expanding model of the universe had essentially proven the creation story in the book of Genesis.

WHERE THERE'S A WILL

Said Hoyle, you quote
Lemaitre, I note,
And Gamow. Well, Forget them!
That errant gang
And their Big Bang—
Why aid them and abet them?

BARBARA GAMOW

THE AGNOSTIC, BOMBASTIC and undeniably brilliant astronomer Fred Hoyle was particularly irritated with Lemaître's theory, which he called, dismissively, the "big bang," a label that stuck, despite its questionable origin and childish ring. Hoyle labored, with his colleagues Hermann Bondi and Thomas Gold, to come up with an alternative explanation—one without some magical creation event.

Hoyle and his colleagues developed a strange and speculative but plausibly scientific model of an eternal universe. He later speculated that their inspiration for the unusual theory came from a movie. The strange plot—it was a ghost story—had an ending that was identical to the beginning, in such a way that the story could cycle eternally. The unfolding narrative of the story did not require a beginning or end.

After the movie, Gold speculated that maybe the universe was like this—constantly developing but needing no beginning.[8]

The "steady state theory" they outlined in a series of remarkable papers argued that the universe was *continually* producing matter, and always had been. The theory suggested that matter was produced *steadily* through an unknown process rather than *suddenly* in the beginning, by an unknown process.

As the universe expanded, diluting the distribution of matter, new matter constantly appeared to fill the empty space, like cars on the freeway that come into your lane if you let too much space open up in front of you. This explained how the universe could be infinitely old and not be thinned out to complete emptiness by expansion. The suggestion that matter was continuously created was provocative and controversial, of course, and many cosmologists were skeptical about the theory's apparent need for a constant and magical source of new matter. But the idea was really no different than the suggestion that all the matter was created "in the beginning" at the big bang. Hoyle and his colleagues, who didn't wear priestly collars, simply replaced Lemaître's big miracle in the beginning with a continuous series of tiny miracles. Whether or not this was less supernatural is a matter of opinion.

Figure 4.7. Fred Hoyle (1915-2001), whose brash, brilliant and sometimes incredibly wrong ideas played a major role in twentieth century cosmology. (Donald D. Clayton/AIP Emilio Segre Visual Archives, Clayton Collection)

Astronomy books from the early 1960s list both Lemaître's big bang and Hoyle's steady state as two candidates for a theory of the origin of the universe. Neither had been confirmed by the tried and true method of making a stunning prediction, and it seemed unlikely that the speculative, sparsely populated field of cosmology was likely to do much better. This changed dramatically in 1965 when two scientists at Bell Labs stumbled across an unknown source of radiation coming from everywhere.

THE RADIATION FROM EVERYWHERE

*If I would be a young man again and had to decide how to make my living,
I would not try to become a scientist or scholar or teacher. I would rather choose
to be a plumber or a peddler in the hope to find that modest degree of
independence still available under present circumstances.*

Albert Einstein

Arno Penzias and Robert Wilson were bringing a radio telescope on line in Murray Hill, New Jersey, home of AT&T's world-
famous Bell Labs. The plan was to point the telescope at the heavens
in the hopes of detecting interesting sources of radio waves "out there."
The universe was now known to be filled with far more than stars
and planets, and one way to catalog the cosmic flora and fauna was to
look for different sources of radiation—gamma, x-ray, ultraviolet,
radio, infrared as well as the traditional visible radiation that Galileo
put to such good use. Penzias and Wilson found an odd source of
radio waves that seemed like it was coming from everywhere. This
was so puzzling that they initially concluded it must be coming from
inside the telescope, where some pigeons had taken up residence and
deposited copious quantities of what they later called a "white dielec-
tric substance" everywhere.

After cleaning the telescope the signal was unchanged, and they
were soon forced to conclude the signal was coming from the sky, but
somehow from *everywhere* in the sky—it did not seem to be originating
at any source like a distant galaxy or star. Penzias and Wilson headed
up the road to Princeton University for a chat with Robert Dicke, a
leading cosmologist, to discuss this odd radiation from everywhere.
Dicke informed them they had just made the most extraordinary of
discoveries; in fact, they had scooped him, as he was just ramping up to
go looking for this radiation from everywhere.

The radiation from everywhere that Penzias and Wilson discovered
had, amazingly, been predicted in 1948 by George Gamow, an eccentric cosmologist who had escaped from Stalinist Russia. Gamow was
something of an anti-Lemaître who drank heavily and loved riding his

motorcycle at great speeds into gatherings of his colleagues. He had speculated, along the same lines as Lemaître, that the universe must have originated in an explosion. But Gamow—who liked Lemaître personally but hated his religion—believed the explosion must have originated from a much hotter state than Lemaître suggested.

Gamow derived a prediction from his "hot" big bang model: the universe, he said, should be filled with a highly specific radiation pattern that would have been released in the early stages of the big bang. Since this radiation would have been everywhere and had no way to

Figure 4.8. The now-famous antenna used by Penzias and Wilson to discover the universal background radiation left over from the big bang. (Fabioj/Wikimedia Commons)

escape from the universe, it must still be here. Gamow specified the precise characteristics of the radiation, the discovery of which would serve as a possible confirmation of the big bang and refutation of the steady state theory. At the time, nobody had the slightest clue how one might go about detecting such incredibly faint radiation.

As often happens, the advance of technology proved beneficial to science, in addition to scientific advance producing new technology.

The telescope that Bell Labs had commissioned was a new technology with unprecedented ability to detect the weak radio waves left over from the big bang. Just as Hubble's telescope had discovered the expanding universe in 1927 so the telescope built by Penzias and Wilson confirmed the big bang theory four decades later.

Within a few years the steady state theory was demoted in astronomy textbooks from a minority viewpoint to a historical footnote of the sort assigned to Aristotle's ideas—historically interesting but no longer scientifically relevant.

Cosmology came to life in the wake of the confirmation of the big bang theory. A field considered so speculative that few ambitious young scientists were attracted to it had just had a foundation laid under it. The universe had an age. The universe had a beginning. But most important for science, the universe had a *history*.

A BRIEF HISTORY OF EVERYTHING

I also think we need to maintain distinctions—the doctrine of creation
is different from a scientific cosmology, and we should resist the temptation,
which sometimes scientists give in to, to try to assimilate
the concepts of theology to the concepts of science.

JOHN POLKINGHORNE

THE COSMIC NARRATIVE of the universe has been written over the past century. Or perhaps we should say it has been written over the past 14 billion years and *deciphered* in the last century. The story is remarkable, illuminating basic questions about the origins of the planets, as well as the orderly way they orbit about the sun. We understand that our sun is an ideal but not unusual star. Its lifetime is about ten billion years, only half of which is used up at present. Our Milky Way galaxy is also quite ordinary, but serves as a stable galactic home for our solar system. The universe itself is around 14 billion years old.

We have deciphered this history in part by looking backward in time. When we look *out* into the universe we look *back* into the past. The light from the sun, for example, takes eight minutes to reach earth.

If you glance at the sun you are seeing it as it was eight minutes ago. When you look at the star system Alpha Centauri, you are seeing stars as they were a few years ago. The picture of the Hyades that Eddington took in 1919 was of stars from a few centuries ago. Because it takes light so long to get to the earth, many things that we "see" on any given night are actually images from long ago. The radiation from the gamma ray burster we met in the introduction brought news of an explosion that occurred billions of years ago.

We can actually look back billions of years into the past and see the

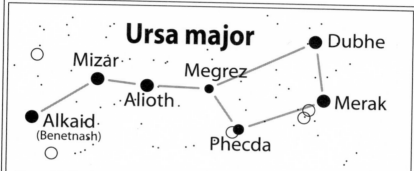

Figure 4.9. The familiar Big Dipper constellation looks like a two-dimensional structure with all the stars the same distance away. Mizar, however, is 78 light years from the sun, and Alioth is 81 light years away, which means that Mizar is trillions of miles farther away than Alioth. (Luigi Chiesa/Wikimedia Commons)

universe as it was even before our solar system existed. The radiation that Penzias and Wilson detected in 1965 was from an event that occurred more than 13 billion years ago.

We decipher the history of our universe by combining many different lines of evidence, all of which have converged on the following remarkable picture, which will be unfolded in more detail in the chapters to follow.

Nobody understands how our universe began. We have no theories that explain it and no observations of what it looked like when it began—if we can even say that it "looked" like anything. But we do have solid theories backed up by observations for the history of the universe from just moments after the big bang. The story goes like this.

In the early universe two kinds of charged particles emerged out of

the great energy of the big bang—*quarks* and *electrons*.[9] The quarks
quickly combined into protons and neutrons, under the constraints of
preexisting laws that told them what to do. And then single protons
paired with neutrons to create the nuclear bundle at the heart of the
hydrogen atom—the nucleus. These nuclei then combined with the
electrons to make atoms. In the earliest phase of the universe there were
no atoms at all—just quarks and electrons. As the universe cooled, all
the matter was gathered into atoms—mostly hydrogen and a bit of helium. Heavier atoms did not form because it was too hard to get multiple protons into the same nucleus because they repel each other very
strongly when they are close together. The early universe thus had no
carbon, oxygen, nitrogen, gold or silver. Both theory and observation
support this picture of the early universe. And if we create a theoretical
model of the big bang, it predicts that the initial energy is not great
enough to produce many atoms heavier than helium.

The early universe is thus rather boring, until gravity comes to the
rescue by gently tugging on the hydrogen and helium atoms until they
gather into huge clouds. These clouds get larger and larger and become
stars as the matter gets compressed into huge balls. Eventually the gravity of these stars becomes so strong that they crush the very atoms of
which they are made. The temperatures rise dramatically until the energy is so great that it rips the electrons from the atoms, which are then
just nuclei. This gravitational crushing process forces the nuclei together
until the star ignites through the process known as *fusion*. Stars shine via
nuclear explosions that last for billions of years. The simple hydrogen
nuclei are compressed so powerfully that they combine into larger nuclei, like little gobs of mercury joining together into a bigger gob. The
larger nuclei in the universe today—carbon, nitrogen, oxygen, iron, gold
and silver—were fused in these ancient furnaces.

As fusion reactions in stars convert hydrogen into heavier nuclei, the
stars get steadily denser, like a snowball being packed from a bunch of
fluffy snow. Because fusion is truly an ongoing nuclear explosion, there is
enough power for a star to explode when it reaches a certain density. The
explosion of a star is an awesome event, as you might imagine. Often the
star about to explode is invisible and just suddenly appears from nowhere

in the sky when it gets incredibly bright by exploding. This was the case with the new star that Tycho Brahe saw to his amazement in 1572.

The explosion of a star creates a huge cloud of material billions of miles in diameter. The cloud will typically be rotating, since most stars rotate, including those that blow up. Much of the cloud will be hydrogen, the predominant component of the star. But there will also be lots of the heavier elements in the cloud as well. The temperatures in the cloud will have dropped dramatically, which allows the free electrons to join the nuclei so that normal atoms come to dominate, just as they did in the early universe (see insert figure G).

Not surprisingly, the omnipresent gravity goes to work on this huge rotating cloud. In the ultimate recycling project, gravity gathers the material in the cloud into concentrated balls. The largest ball is at the center and the smaller balls orbit about it. The central ball, of course, is a star in the making. The smaller balls are planets, many with moons forming about them. As the huge cloud rotates, the balls that form naturally orbit about the central sun in the same direction. And the rotation flattens the cloud, just as the earth is flattened a bit by its rotation. The flattening results in the planets orbiting about the sun in almost the same plane, like runners on the same track.

IN THE BEGINNING GOD CREATED

For the scientist who has lived by his faith in the power of reason, the story ends like a bad dream. He has scaled the mountains of ignorance; he is about to conquer the highest peak; as he pulls himself over the final rock, he is greeted by a band of theologians who have been sitting there for centuries.

Robert Jastrow

THE COSMIC NARRATIVE is a long, long story from the big bang to the present. The creative capacities of the universe are mind-boggling. To get a solar system like ours out of a boring universe populated only by hydrogen and helium atoms is quite an achievement. There is absolutely nothing of interest to make from hydrogen and helium. Hydrogen atoms can pair up to form a molecule, which is hardly exciting—

and that is it. And helium can't do anything, in the absence of a balloon and a child to play with it. Imagine, if you will, looking at a big pile of Legos, with only two different sized blocks—no wheels, no interesting corners or rounded pieces, no roofing or foundation plates. What could possibly be constructed from such limited raw materials?

And yet here we are 13 billion years later on a remarkable planet orbiting at just the right distance from the right kind of star. Our solar system is relatively free of wayward asteroids and debris that could be smashing into us. Our planetary orbit is nearly circular, so the surface temperatures of our planet remain relatively constant. Our star is stable, with a near constant output of energy, quite remarkable when you realize that a star is basically a gigantic ongoing nuclear explosion.

Our planet has generous quantities of water—but not so much that there is no dry land. And most of this water is in liquid form, distributed over almost the entire surface of the planet. This is far more significant than most people realize. We take liquid water for granted. After all, we can turn a faucet and a seemingly endless supply comes running out. We let it run down the drain while we wait for it to get colder or hotter or whatever temperature we prefer.

Liquid water is so rare in the universe that an inventory of the entire contents of the universe would probably omit it entirely—just as an inventory of your household possessions would omit pennies that fell between the cushions on your sofa, or returnable bottles in the garage or dust bunnies under your bed. H_2O in *any* form is quite rare, but the liquid form is almost nonexistent. Most places—like the space between the stars—are way too cold and H_2O would be in the form of ice. And the places that are not too cold—like stars—are way too hot. A narrow range of temperatures where water can be a liquid is found only on planets orbiting at just the right distance from their suns.

Water, of course, is the liquid of life. Life cannot even be imagined in the absence of water. Life also needs other special conditions and a roster of complicated molecules that are also rare. Worlds without the long roster of necessary conditions, which are hard to even specify since we don't know how life began, are barren and sterile. And this would describe most of the worlds orbiting their various stars.

The history that proceeds from the big bang to our remarkable planet is most curious in the way it has provided liquid water, a stable sun and all the chemicals necessary for life. This unusual history gives the unmistakable impression that the story of the universe is *our* story—that we belong here. We are not, as some uninspired secular prophets would have us believe, glorious accidents.

LIVING ON A
GOLDILOCKS PLANET

Why the Earth Is Such a Great Place to Live

God is infinite, so His universe must be too. Thus is the excellence
of God magnified and the greatness of His kingdom made manifest;
He is glorified not in one, but in countless suns; not in a single
earth, a single world, but in a thousand thousand, I say in an in-
finity of worlds.

GIORDANO BRUNO

ABOUT TWENTY LIGHT YEARS—120 trillion miles—from
earth, in the constellation Libra, a planet named Gliese 581g orbits a
star resembling our sun. It's the fourth planet out from the star, which
can only be seen from earth with a telescope. Not far from the middle
of its solar system, comfortably situated in what astronomers call the
"Goldilocks Zone," the planet is not too hot and not too cold, but "just
right," like the porridge in the fairy tale. Its gravity is also not too
strong and not too weak, so it could have a stable atmosphere like
earth. And its star is not too bright and not too dim.

Gliese 581g orbits about its sun in the middle of what astronomers
call the *habitable zone*. Five hundred other planets have been discovered
to date outside our solar system, and this is the first one that might be
habitable. It is also nearby—at least by astronomical standards—being

located in our galactic neighborhood. A huge spaceship traveling over the lifetime of many generations of astronauts could conceivably get there, although the expense would be so great as to essentially render the project impossible.

Astronomers have waxed eloquent about 581g. One of the discoverers called it "Zarmina's World," after his wife, convinced that such a "beautiful planet" deserves a more interesting name than "581g."[1] A Penn State astronomer, enthused at the prospects of extraterrestrial life, says Zarmina's World is the "first one I'm truly excited about." After decades of finding uninhabitable sterile orbs, this discovery has finally provided a license to think seriously—or at least scientifically—about the prospects that we are not alone in the universe (see insert figure H).

The hypothetical citizens on Zarmina's World have already been embraced by the Catholic Church as "children of God." An official Vatican astronomer, Jesuit priest José Gabriel Funes, finds nothing surprising in the prospects of extraterrestrial life: "Just as there is a multiplicity of creatures on Earth, so there could be other beings created by God." Another Vatican astronomer-priest assures us that the Zarminians would have souls, and says he would be happy to baptize them, "if they asked."[2]

Theologically conservative Protestant Ken Ham, head of the creationist organization Answers in Genesis, disagrees. He claims that the Vatican astronomers' offers to baptize the Zarminians shows that they "can't truly understand the gospel." "The Bible," says Ham, "makes it clear that Adam's sin affected the whole universe. This means that any aliens would also be affected by Adam's sin, but they can't have salvation. . . . [T]o suggest that aliens could respond to the gospel is just totally wrong."[3]

All this fussing and fretting about aliens might lead one to believe that some sort of signal had been received—an unmistakably intelligent message like what Jodie Foster's character, astronomer Ellie Arroway, deciphered in the move *Contact*. The great distance to the planet rules out the possibility of actual alien Zarminians being among us, but a mere twenty light years is no barrier to radio transmission. If the Zarminians started twenty years ago broadcasting messages to earth, or even generically in all directions, we would be receiving them by now. Radio waves have, in fact, been emanating from earth in all directions for almost a century and could be detected by any extraterrestrial civilization with the appropriate technology. But we are receiving no radio messages from 581g or any other planet in the universe. So why all the excitement about the Zarminians?

HOPE SPRINGS ETERNAL

Our Moon exists for us on the earth, not for the other globes.
Those four little moons exist for Jupiter, not for us. . . . From this line of reason
we deduce with the highest degree of probability that Jupiter is inhabited.

JOHANNES KEPLER

ZARMINA'S WORLD, AS near as we can tell, is not like the earth. Astronomers have not "beamed down" on a planet with breathable air, familiar gravity and comfortable temperatures, as Captain Kirk and the crew of the Starship Enterprise were constantly doing on *Star Trek*. We now know that the vast majority of planets are nothing like those convenient Hollywood fantasies.

Zarmina's World is three times the mass of the earth but only slightly larger, so gravity would be much stronger there, due to the greatly increased density. Upon being beamed onto that surface Captain Kirk would find himself weighing over 500 pounds, posing challenges for his trademark brawls with the local aliens. In fact, he would have trouble even standing upright, seriously compromising the charismatic persona that always seemed so appealing to the local alien females (see insert figure I).

Zarmina's World is much closer to its star than our earth is to the sun—14 million miles compared to 93 million for the earth. Its "year" is just 37 days long. It rotates so slowly that one side almost always faces the sun, creating temperatures as hot as 160 degrees—beyond even the most dreadful spots on the surface of the earth. The dark side is like the Canadian winters I enjoyed as a boy: -25°F (that's below zero!). In the literal twilight zone between the unbearable heat and the Canadian cold would be some pleasant temperatures, where creatures like us could certainly make ourselves at home. Zarminians, if they exist, would have to move every so often as the planet slowly turned, to remain in the temperate zone where water could easily be maintained in liquid form.

The hopeful, even confident, speculations that there might be life on Zarmina's World reveal just how eager astronomers—and many other members of our species—are to discover that we are not the only life in this big universe. Vogt, codiscoverer of the planet, and the earthling Zarmina's husband—Mr. Zarmina—believes that "chances for life on this planet are 100 percent." Vogt's speculation, alas, is one part science and ninety-nine parts wishful thinking: Zarmina's World has *some* surface area between 32°F and 212°F (0°–100° C). So, in the event that water exists in those regions—which we don't know—it would be liquid. And water is essential for life. Therefore, there *could* be life on Zarmina's World—which is more than you can say for the hundreds of other planets that have been discovered outside our solar system.

We don't know if Zarmina's World actually has any water, but the chances are reasonable based on what we know about water in the universe in general. Whether that water has contributed to the formation of life is an entirely different question. What these speculations about life in Zarminian waters remind us is how critically important and unusual our water supply is here on the earth—a cosmic quirk that we take for granted. There is an inextricable link between liquid water and life, both here on the earth and anywhere else in the universe we hope life might exist.

WATER, WATER, EVERYWHERE—OR NOT

And there sat Sam, looking cool and calm, in the heart of the furnace roar;
And he wore a smile you could see a mile, and he said: "Please close that door.
It's fine in here, but I greatly fear you'll let in the cold and storm—
Since I left Plumtree, down in Tennessee, it's the first time I've been warm."

ROBERT SERVICE, "THE CREMATION OF SAM McGEE"

ALMOST THREE-FOURTHS OF the surface of the earth is covered with water, and virtually all of the world's cities are on a body of water. Most people live near rivers, lakes and oceans. And water even makes up 60 percent of the human body, a fact readily apparent when one is sweating in the hot sun or desperately thirsty.

Water, in many parts of the world, seems almost magically available. It pours from our taps on demand, falls from the sky, bubbles up in springs, cascades down the sides of mountains and over cliffs. We swim in it, bathe in it, run it through hoses to water our lawns or entertain our children. We make ice from it to put in our drinks. We skate on it. Even beavers use it freely and recklessly, creating gigantic ponds in which to raise their families. In those many parts of the world blessed with an abundance of water, we take it for granted.

In the larger universe, however, water is rare (see insert figure J). In some ways the universe seems so inhospitable to liquid water that one might infer that water is not welcome.

For starters, the temperatures don't cooperate. All but an insignificant fraction of the volume of space is essentially empty. The volume taken up by stars, planets, moons, comets and other bodies where water might possibly be found is quite insignificant. And all this empty space is cold—really cold.

Growing up in Canada I learned a lot about cold. In the midst of winter, during my teen years, I arose before dawn to deliver my village's only daily newspaper, the *Telegraph Journal*. The thermometer outside our kitchen window was a stark and skinny messenger framed against the darkness, feebly illuminated by light from inside the house. The mercury on many mornings all but vanished into the little ball at the bottom of the thermometer, with temperatures reading -40°F (Canada had not yet gone metric). The weather report on the radio would warn that additional chilling from the wind had reduced that temperature even further, sometimes to more than -60°F. Dressed warmly by my thoroughly Canadian mother and with one of her hand-knit woolen scarves about my mouth, I would head out into the pitch-black frigid morning to deliver the news to the good citizens of the little village of Bath, New Brunswick. I would return an hour later, an icicle several inches long hanging from the scarf in front of my mouth, where my breath had condensed and frozen in the cold air.

A decade later I found myself studying at Rice University in Houston, Texas, where thermometers had no need for negative numbers. I arrived in the middle of August and was greeted by temperatures that routinely exceeded 100 degrees, a dreadful situation made even worse by high humidity and requiring the continuous use of air conditioners. In between the extremes of New Brunswick and Texas lie the narrow temperatures that humans enjoy—85 degrees at the beach, 72 in our offices, 65 on a pleasant evening as we turn in for the night.

The temperature ranges experienced by humans seem extreme but that is simply our limited and parochial view. Those cold temperatures that greeted me as I headed out on frosty Canadian mornings are positively balmy compared to the average temperature of the universe, which is more than 400 degrees cooler. If you took a space voyage to another star system, the temperature outside your window for most of the long journey would be -454°F. A cold Canadian winter would be a welcome relief from such unimaginable cold. On the other hand, the temperature on the stars runs as high as 70,000 degrees, an inferno capable of melting just about anything. You would be incinerated just by getting too close, never mind actually making physical contact.

The temperature range where humans feel comfortable is thus *extremely* narrow compared to the universe as a whole. And even the larger range where humans can exist—the habitable zone—is very narrow.

Water seems even more remarkable when we note that only 5 percent of the total matter in the universe is the ordinary familiar stuff made up of atoms and molecules. The other 95 percent consists of largely unknown stuff called, for lack of better terms, *dark matter* and *dark energy*. All the elements on the chemists' periodic table, all the vast collection of atoms and molecules that comprise the earth, the sun and the other planets, all the stars in the Milky Way galaxy—all this matter is less than 5 percent of the total stuff in the universe.[4] And this small percentage is itself composed almost entirely of hydrogen, with water making up but a small fraction. Water thus comprises much less than 1 percent of the universe. Given that water accounts for two-thirds of the matter in our bodies, we can see that we are most unusual from a purely chemical point of view, not to mention our more remarkable characteristics.

THE LONG AND WINDING STREAM

The winds, the sea, and the moving tides are what they are.
If there is wonder and beauty and majesty in them, science will discover
these qualities. If they are not there, science cannot create them.

RACHEL CARSON

WATER GETS EVEN more interesting when we look at the history of how it got to the earth. The story begins with the big bang, the cosmic fireball we met earlier.

Popular views of the big bang picture all the matter in the universe exploding outward like something blowing up in an action movie. This original matter then combined into the cosmic structures we find in the universe today. This picture is way too simple.

The big bang produced no matter. Only unimaginably high *energies* emerged from that mysterious and transcendent event. Picture the energy released as an atomic bomb explodes; now multiply this many times over. These energies were so high that matter simply could not exist. Of course, there was no such thing as matter in the universe then, so this statement is a bit odd.

A universe with no matter in it would remain quite uninteresting, but fortunately the universe was born with a set of remarkable physical laws. One of the most basic of those laws was discovered by Albert Einstein in 1905: $E=mc^2$.

This law is the most well-known equation in all of science. Most people don't know any equations at all, but if they do know one, it is $E=mc^2$. It has graced the covers of magazines, T-shirts and posters. It inspired the atomic bomb, nuclear reactors and dreams of unlimited free energy from seawater. And most important, it was the door through which matter entered our universe.

As the early universe expanded, it cooled, following the same laws of physics running your refrigerator. Cooling is simply the name we give to a decrease in the energy content of a region of space, whether it is your freezer, a Canadian winter or the entire universe. Any quantity of energy will have to decrease in temperature if it spreads out to fill a larger volume. This is why opening your door in the winter cools your house—some of the heat energy flows out the door, futilely trying to warm up the front yard.

Figure 5.1. Hungarian refugee and physicist Leo Szilard convinced Albert Einstein to draft a letter to President Roosevelt recommending that the United States start working on an atomic bomb, based on Einstein's famous equation describing how energy could be extracted from matter: $E=mc^2$. Conversely, it also shows that that great energies could produce matter. This is what happened shortly after the eruption of the big bang. (U.S. Department of Energy/Wikimedia Commons)

As the early universe expanded and cooled it reached critical temperatures where interesting things happened, like when water cools and freezes. If you were swimming under water that was about to freeze—hopefully in a wetsuit to keep you from also freezing—you would see ice crystals suddenly appearing, seemingly out of nowhere. Small bits of water would suddenly be transformed into slivers of ice. Liquid would have become solid. This is what water does as it cools. In the same way, as the early universe cooled, matter popped into existence.

Matter first appeared in two forms—the familiar *electrons*, with negative electrical charges, and the less familiar *quarks* with electrical charges of 2/3 and –1/3. Quarks are odd particles conceived in the 1960s to explain the peculiar behavior of other particles. One of their many odd properties is that—like teenagers at the mall—they are never found alone. As soon as they appear, they immediately combine with each other. But they don't just combine—they form specific particles

Figure 5.2. When water is cooled to the freezing point, crystals of ice pop into existence, seemingly out of nowhere. This is called a *phase transition* and is a good analogy to material particles popping into existence in the early universe as it cooled. (Mila Zinkova/Wikimedia Commons)

that have total electrical charges of either 1 or 0. The most familiar examples of particles with these charges are the proton and neutron, respectively, but there are others. One curious result of this rule of combination is that we *never* encounter particles with fractional charges, even though we know that both protons and neutrons are composed of particles with fractional charges. In the early days, before this odd rule was understood, heroic efforts were mounted to find a fractionally charged quark hanging out by itself, but none were discovered. Eventually the theory came to include a rule precluding lone-ranger quarks.

After the quarks combine in the early universe, the newly minted matter consists of protons, neutrons and electrons buzzing about in a chaotic but steadily cooling mix. The particles move at great speeds but gradually slow down as the universe expands and cools. Positively charged protons attract negatively charged electrons. As soon as the speeds get low enough—which occurs at a specific temperature—the electron drops into an orbit about a proton, like a child leaping onto a spinning merry-go-round when it slows down enough. The neutrons occasionally bang into protons and stick there, forming the combination still found today in the nucleus of a hydrogen atom. The universe is now full of hydrogen atoms, with a few helium atoms leavening the mixture.

All the particles in the universe are now electrically neutral atoms—their negatively charged electrons balance their positively charged protons. The powerful electrical forces of attraction and repulsion no longer dominate, and the much weaker gravitational force takes over. The brand new hydrogen atoms float freely about but gravity gathers them ever so slowly together. Clouds of hydrogen gradually form, growing ever larger, and as they get larger they pull with more gravitational force on other atoms. Eventually much of the hydrogen is collected into huge steadily growing clouds that surpass the size of the moon, then the earth, then a large planet like Jupiter. As the clouds get larger they become more compressed, their gravity growing ever stronger.

Nothing limits how strong gravity can become. Eventually another threshold is crossed and the hydrogen atoms become so densely compacted they actually fuse together in a nuclear reaction. This fusion ignites the gigantic balls of hydrogen and, like a slow-motion fireworks display, great spheres of hydrogen turn into stars. Unfortunately, there are no life forms in the universe to witness this extraordinary display, especially since this turns out be a critical step in preparing the universe for life. But amazingly the images of these fireworks end up traveling for billions of years across the universe and are eventually observed, long after the events have faded into history.

The gravity within these newly born stars crushes the hydrogen nuclei, fusing them into helium nuclei and giving off great quantities of light and heat. The process begins to fill the blanks on the periodic table of the elements. Two hydrogens make helium. Add one more and we have lithium. Two helium make beryllium. Add another and we have carbon. Other combinations make nitrogen, oxygen, neon, sodium and on down the periodic table.

At this point the universe is billions of years old and still without an isolated drop of water anywhere. No stars have planets orbiting them, and no solid surfaces exist anywhere on which one could stand. The raw materials out of which planets and people will eventually be constructed are buried deep inside brightly shining stars, and if this were where it ended, there would be nobody to lament our brightly glowing but failed and stillborn universe. But there are more chapters to the story, as you might have anticipated, based on the simple fact that you exist.

GOING OUT WITH A BANG

*Amazed, and as if astonished and stupefied, I stood still, gazing for a certain
length of time with my eyes fixed intently upon it and noticing that same
star placed close to the stars which antiquity attributed to Cassiopeia.
When I had satisfied myself that no star of that kind had ever shone
forth before, I was led into such perplexity by the unbelievability
of the thing that I began to doubt the faith of my own eyes.*

TYCHO BRAHE

LARGE STARS NEAR the end of their lives regularly explode as a
matter of course. With the force of a billion atomic bombs they strew
their contents over unimaginably vast regions of space. It is, of course,
a once-in-a-lifetime event for the star—a literal going out with a bang.
And even though recorded history is just a few thousand years long—
and stars live for billions of years—we have some examples of such explosions that were noted by careful observers.

In A.D. 1054 what is now the Crab Nebula exploded in a flash of
light bright enough to be seen in daylight for weeks. Observers in Korea,
China, Japan, North America and the Middle East all recorded the
supernova, as it is now called, although Europeans did not. It seems
that Europeans, convinced that the heavens were perfect and unchanging, managed to delude themselves into not seeing this new star, which
must surely have been quite visible (see insert figure K).

The great Danish astronomer Tycho Brahe witnessed another supernova in 1572. Like his predecessors, he could not believe that such
a dramatic change in the heavens was possible, but, apparently unlike
his predecessors, he had enough confidence in his observations to know
that he was seeing something remarkable. Brahe's protégé, Johannes
Kepler, witnessed another supernova in 1604, and then there were no
more visible from earth until 1987, when a star exploded in a nearby
galaxy known as the Large Magellanic Cloud.

A supernova explosion fills a massive region of space with the elements created inside the star; the powerful explosion, though, follows
known laws of physics as it distributes its contents about the universe.

Figure A. Lucas van Valckenborch imagined the Tower of Babel with its top reaching toward the heavens. (Lucas van Valckenborch/Wikimedia Commons)

Figure B. The curved shadow cast by the earth on the moon during a solar eclipse was one of several observations that convinced the Greeks, centuries before Christ, that the earth must be round and not flat. Very few thinkers during the Christian era believed the earth was flat, contrary to popular mythology. (Riyaz Ahamed/Wikipedia)

Figure C. Viewed from the outer reaches of the solar system, the earth appears as a speck of dust, a sobering and humbling reminder of the scale of the universe. (NASA/JPL)

Figure D. An artist's conception of the Milky Way, if we could get "above" it and look down. Our solar system is located near the end of one of the spiral arms. There are approximately two hundred billion stars in the Milky Way. (NASA/JPL-Caltech)

Figure E. The atmosphere, clouds and water (visible in this famous photo from Apollo 17) are all held on the earth by gravity. Solid material is heaviest so the water sits on top of the land. Air and clouds are located above the water for the same reason. (NASA)

Figure F. Dante's *Divine Comedy* was based on the pre-Copernican view that hell was at the center of the earth. Dante's levels in hell reflected the widespread belief that the center of the earth was the worst place in the universe. Things improved as you proceeded out from there until you reached the heavens, where things were perfect. (Sandro Botticelli/Wikimedia Commons)

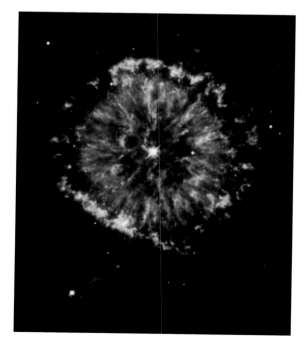

Figure G. This is a picture of "The Glowing Eye" nebula, taken by the Hubble Telescope. A dying star lies in the center, surrounded by a vast cloud of material that has been ejected. (NASA)

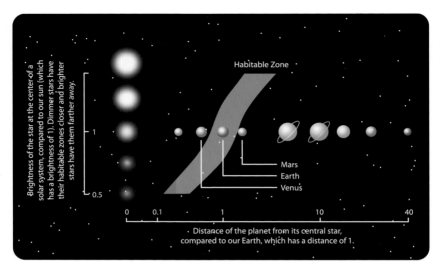

Figure H. This diagram illustrates the principle of a "habitable zone." A planet lying on the wavy diagonal swath would have temperatures permitting liquid water, the most critical prerequisite for life, but far from the only one. The earth is pictured here, at a distance known as one astronomical unit from the sun, which is the star on the left in the middle. For larger stars, like the one on the top left, the habitable zone is farther out. For smaller and cooler stars, like the bottom left, the zone is closer in. Zarmina's world would have to be in the lower part of the habitable swath, since its sun is dimmer than ours.

Figure I. In science fiction stories like the perennially popular Star Trek series, characters are routinely visiting unknown planets that turn out to be so similar to earth that travelers can function—breathe, eat, move about—normally. In reality, the overwhelming majority of planets would be hostile to humans and completely incapable of supporting complex life forms. (Star Trek, season 2, episode 22, originally aired February 16, 1967, Paramount Pictures)

Figure J. The most striking feature of Earth is its water. Viewed from space it seems like a ball of water, which, in many ways, is not a bad description. (NASA)

Figure K. The Crab Nebula is the cloud of debris created when a star exploded in A.D. 1054. Of course it exploded many years earlier but became visible in 1054. The cloud of material that remains is rich in heavier elements. Over the next few million years a solar system will probably form from this nebula. (NASA and ESA/Wikimedia Commons)

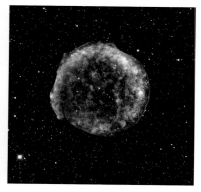

Figure L. The remnant of the supernova that startled the great Danish astronomer Tycho Brahe in 1572. This entire cloud of material was exploded from a single star. The process made the star so much brighter it was visible during the day. (NASA/MPIA/Calar Alto Observatory, Oliver Krause et al./Wikimedia Commons)

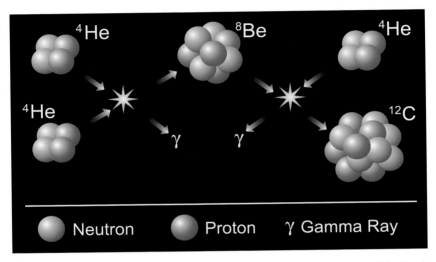

Figure M. This is the spectrum of neon. Each line represents a signature wavelength, ranging from a few short wavelength lines on the left to a lot of longer wavelength lines on the right. The lines in the visible part of the spectrum can be seen directly, but most of them are invisible—infrared, ultraviolet, x-ray and so on. If a spectrum like this is observed from an unknown gas in a distant part of the universe, we know with certainty that it is being produced by neon. (Jan Homann/Wikimedia Commons)

Figure N. The fusion reaction that produces the element carbon. The energy of the Beryllium (^{8}Be) and helium (^{4}He) nuclei together are a perfect match for an energy level in the carbon atom, making the process surprisingly efficient. The gamma rays are released energy.

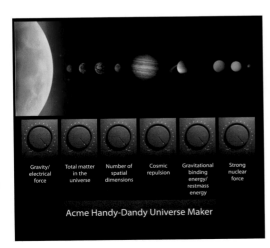

Figure O. In Sir Martin Rees' delightful survey, *Just Six Numbers*, he identifies six specific numerical relationships that are responsible for most of the structure of the universe. Tweaking any of these "knobs" results in large changes over the history of the universe. Almost any departure from the actual settings of the knobs—the specific values we find in our universe—will change the universe in a way that would make life, at least as we know it, impossible.

Figure P. Newton could see no reason why the planets were all in the same plane and traveling in the same direction, so he inferred that this was the handiwork of God. Laplace showed that solar systems (an artist's conception here of ours that is not to scale) naturally form this way from rotating clouds of stardust. (NASA)

Figure Q. Artist's conception of the asteroid striking the Yucatan peninsula 65 million years ago, leaving a vast crater that geologists discovered in the late twentieth century. Evidence suggests that this catastrophic event altered the earth's climate and drove the dinosaurs to extinction. (Donald E. Davis/NASA)

Figures R-S. Snow, especially for Canadians like myself, provides a unique insight into the beauty of the world. On a large scale, snowfalls and especially drifts formed by snow falling in the wind are incredibly beautiful. On a small scale, individual snowflakes have a beautiful symmetry of their own. And, on an abstract level, the molecular structure that creates the amazing geometry of a snowflake is yet another level of beauty. (Snowdrift: Svickova/Wikimedia Commons; Snowflake: U.S. Department of Agriculture/Wikimedia Commons)

A vast cloud of chemically enriched material, trillions of miles in diameter, results from the event—an event absolutely critical for enabling life (see insert figure L).

The grand cloud that results from the supernova resembles the original cloud out of which the star formed in the first place, with one important difference—it contains a substantial roster of different materials, and not just hydrogen and helium. This time around gravity has more to work with, beginning again to gather the material in the huge cloud back into balls. The largest chunk at the center becomes another star—one that starts out with heavier elements, in addition to hydrogen. It is the ultimate recycling project, but unlike recycling on earth, the atoms getting recycled remain in mint condition, no matter how many times they are used.

Some of the smaller balls end up orbiting about the second-generation star. These smaller balls contain many different atoms, and some of them have a curious molecular combination of hydrogen and oxygen. In most parts of the universe these molecules are in the form of a solid. In the others they are a gas. But on balls that are exactly the right distance from the central star, the molecules are liquid, an all-purpose, seemingly magical liquid called *water*.

Water is found in several places in our solar system. Hydrogen is, of course, the most common element in the universe, and while oxygen is less common it is readily available to combine with hydrogen and form water. Water in the form of ice is a major component in comets and can be found in trace quantities in the atmosphere of Venus, under the surface of Mars and possibly even on some of Jupiter's moons.

(We have to keep in mind, however, that more than 99 percent of the mass of the solar system is in the sun, so the distribution of elements elsewhere is almost irrelevant from the perspective of the solar system as a whole. The earth has a lot of water, but the earth is a tiny, insignificant speck compared to the sun. And because the water tends to cover so much of the surface, it is easy to overestimate the total amount. Astronomers are not sure exactly where the water on the earth came from. Constructing the early history of our solar system is an enormous challenge.)

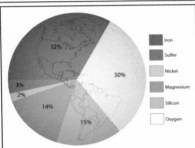

Figure 5.3. Composition of the earth. The composition of the earth differs greatly from that of the sun, which is mostly hydrogen. The differing composition of objects in the solar system is largely due to the different temperatures of the region about the sun when they formed. Heavy elements like iron are easily gathered into planets in hot regions where water would be a gas and tend to escape the weak gravity of the planet.

From a purely scientific point of view, water is a molecule like any other—and there are lots of molecules. The laws of physics and chemistry describe its behavior, and there are no deep mysteries embedded in its familiar structure. But the laws of physics and chemistry conspire to make water unusual in ways that are critically important for life. Most peculiarly, water expands rather than contracts when it freezes. This makes ice lighter than water, so it floats. Floating ice insulates the water beneath it from the cold temperatures of winter. Absent this layer of insulation bodies of water all over the earth would freeze solid. If ice were heavier than water, the layer of ice that formed on the top would sink to the bottom and another layer would freeze on top and sink until the entire body of water was a solid piece of ice. This would kill almost every life form in the water.

Water is also an effective solvent. Waste products from our bodies dissolve readily in water and can then easily be expelled. But wait—as they say on television—there is more. Water is also a remarkable coolant capable of absorbing heat and carrying it away from our bodies in the form of sweat. And water stores heat in our bodies, helping keep us warm in cold weather. Magical.

THE GATHERING OF THE WATERS

If anyone gives even a cup of cold water to one of these little ones because he is my disciple, I tell you the truth, he will certainly not lose his reward.

MATTHEW 10:42 NIV

THE CREATION STORY in Genesis records that God gathered the waters. In the King James Version that I read as a child it says, "God said, Let the waters under the heaven be gathered together unto one place, and let the dry land appear: and it was so." In ways that the original readers of Genesis could never have imagined, the gathering of the waters was a cosmic process that took billions of years and involved all the laws of physics and chemistry. The water that we take for granted that covers so much of our planet and makes up so much of our bodies was forged in the nuclear furnace of a star that exploded in the suburbs of the Milky Way galaxy billions of years ago.

That water now cycles endlessly through the life process here on earth—cooling, cleansing and nurturing us. It irrigates our crops, nourishes our livestock, cleans our clothes and gets turned into snow at ski resorts. In those parts of the world where it is plentiful, clean and fresh, we take it for granted and play with it. In Quebec City they construct a hotel out of ice every winter to attract tourists and invite hardy souls to hold their weddings there, wearing parkas and snow boots. We think nothing of using thousand of gallons so our lawns will be green rather than brown in the heat of summer. Water is like air—plentiful and useful.

Figure 5.4. Children acquire fresh water from a pump in Bulawayo, Zimbabwe. As part of its Water and Sanitation project, World Vision in Zimbabwe constructed three water pumps in this village, which help provide the local school and more than 500 households with water. (© 2007 Mary Makharashvili; used courtesy of World Vision)

In parts of the world where fresh water is rare, its value is more apparent. There is a school in Bulawayo, Zimbabwe, where children used to walk a quarter mile during their breaks to get a drink of water. I used to walk to the hallway to get a drink when I was in school. World Vision, one of many organizations helping with water problems around the world, installed a well near the school that the children now use to get water. On school days a group of laughing, happy children can be seen working the oversized pump that takes several of them to manage. The water that emerges from its modest faucet is welcomed in ways that few North Americans can appreciate.

For those schoolchildren the water is simply a welcome part of their diet and lifestyle now. Some of the children that stay in school and go on to university will eventually discover that the precious fluid summoned from beneath the earth by a few children cranking on a lever was created billions of years ago, deep in the heart of a star, via processes of unimaginable subtlety. Those that have learned to worship God will no doubt marvel and give thanks.

Water exists because the universe has a set of laws that guide its steady development from the big bang into the present. If we suppose that water and the life it enables are of no consequence, then we can dismiss these laws as irrelevant. On the other hand, if we believe that God is the Creator of life and that life has a purpose, then these laws take on a new character. If God is the Creator, then these laws exist because God created them. And these laws work because God upholds them from moment to moment. Viewed by these lights, the origin of water and life are creation events, intentionally enabled by the Creator of the universe.

6

MONKEYING WITH
THE PHYSICS

The Wonder of the World Within the World

*I want to know how God created this world. I am not interested in
this or that phenomenon, in the spectrum of this or that element. I
want to know His thoughts. The rest are details.*

ALBERT EINSTEIN

IN 1984 I WAITED IN A LONG LINE in a consulate in Houston,
Texas, to file some paperwork to become a permanent resident of the
United States. Texas consulates are notoriously busy because of the
steady influx of people from Mexico. After several despairing hours in
a line that started outside the building, I got close enough to the front
of the line that hope became a realistic option. When I got within ear-
shot of the window where the elusive immigration transactions took
place I overhead a young man in front of me pleading in desperation
with the bureaucrat in charge. The young man was trying to pay his
filing fee of $20 with a $50 bill. The tired and tedious bureaucrat was
explaining that he had to pay with exact change or write a check. The
young man, who had a stack of $50 bills that I think he would have
been happy to part with *in toto* if it would complete this process, explained that he would forgo any change he had coming if they would
just put his paperwork through. His complaint fell on deaf ears. This

office dealt with *exact* change and *exact* change only. If you had too much or too little, it was all the same—you couldn't file your paperwork. Come back another day and stand in that long line again. Next!

I stepped up and rescued the young man. In exchange for one $50 bill from his stash, I wrote a check for $20 to the U.S. government and a check to the grateful man for $30, all the while fuming about a system that would let someone wait in line for hours and then refuse to take his money because his bills were too large. My good Samaritan act was rewarded when the $30 check I had written to the happy young man was never cashed.

Transactions at that consulate window were precisely specified, and they simply did not occur unless a person exactly matched his or her fee with the payment. Too much or too little and nothing would happen.

Many transactions in nature are exactly like this. The currency is energy, rather than dollars, and the events are physical changes in matter rather than immigration status, but the process is the same: there must be a perfect match between the physical change and the proffered energy or nothing will occur. And there is no analog to a Canadian standing in line behind you creating a loophole.

NATURE'S PUT-UP JOB

A common sense interpretation of the facts suggests that a superintellect has monkeyed with physics, as well as chemistry and biology, and that there are no blind forces worth speaking about in nature.

FRED HOYLE

IN THE LAST chapter we looked at the heroic effort made by the universe to create water and stock the earth with it in liquid form. In this chapter we want to dig deeper and look at the details of the processes that actually produce the water molecules in the first place. We will discover that the laws of nature have a highly specified character that makes this process work. Not only is the process breathtaking on a large scale, as we watch the universe produce hydrogen, stars, heavy elements, water and finally habitable planets, but the process is even more breathtaking when we look more closely at exactly how this is done. The devil—or in this case, God—seems to be in the details.

This part of our story begins in 1950, around the time that the steady state and big bang theories competed for the allegiance of cosmologists. In parallel with those discussions, many of the same physicists were developing theories about how the heavier elements were produced in the stars. It had become clear that the early universe—or the eternal universe for the steady state devotees—contained little more than hydrogen and a bit of helium, in terms of conventional matter. Elements heavier than helium—like carbon, nitrogen, oxygen—had been created in the stars billions of years later. Observations of stars made this crystal clear.

Every element on the periodic table gives off a characteristic radiation pattern when the atom is highly energized. In some cases this can be seen with the naked eye by simply looking at the color of the radiation. So-called neon signs are a perfect example. The ones with actual neon in them are orange. Others are red, blue or green; the gas in the tube determines the exact color. You can identify the gas in the tube from a mile away just by noting its color. If it's orange, it's neon. If it's blue, it's xenon. A scientist would take the observation a few steps further and look more closely at the *spectrum* of the light, noting that each gas gives off many different colors with varying degrees of brightness. What we see with our naked eye is the collection of all the individual colors mixed together to give the impression of one color, like the way a lot of baking ingredients can be mixed into a cake that appears to have just a single taste after the ingredients are combined and baked. The orange color of neon comes from bright lines in the orange part of its spectrum, but there are also lines that are green and blue. The collection of individual colors given off by an atom or molecule is so specific that it is often referred to as an *electromagnetic fingerprint*. Just as your fingerprints are unique to you, so atoms and molecules have unique spectra characteristic to them. The study of spectra is called *spectroscopy* (see insert figure M).

When astronomers examine the light from stars, even those trillions of miles away, they can tell from the radiation given off that there are

certain specific atoms in those stars. Astronomers going back to Newton had been breaking light up into its individual spectral lines, and
even in the nineteenth century, before it was clear to the chemists that
matter was composed of atoms, the spectrum of helium and other elements had been noted in stars. By the 1950s stellar spectroscopy had
identified heavier elements in the stars. And older stars had more heavy
elements than younger ones. This was solid observational evidence that
stars converted light elements into heavy elements as they aged. But
nobody knew how.

The theory of nuclear fusion developed in the early twentieth century provided, in broad brushstrokes, an explanation for how this
worked. Protons and neutrons, if slammed into each other with sufficient force, could join together, or *fuse*, to form composite particles.
The fusing of protons is quite remarkable because they have positive
charges that strongly repel each other, like the matching poles of magnets that fascinate children. But if the protons were moving fast
enough—which means they were very hot and had a lot of energy—
they could overcome their electrical repulsion, contact each other, and
stick together.[1]

(The temperatures at which this occurs are so high that all the electrons have been ripped off the atoms, as I mentioned earlier. So, when
I say hydrogen or helium I am referring only to their nuclei. A normal
hydrogen nucleus is just a proton and a normal helium nucleus contains
two protons and two neutrons. The number of neutrons can vary—
hydrogen can have one or two instead of zero, and helium can have
three instead of two—but the less common combinations—called *isotopes*—are often *unstable* and will spontaneously disintegrate into the
more familiar forms, which are *stable*. The isotope of hydrogen, with
one neutron, is called deuterium and is stable, but the one with two
neutrons, called tritium, is unstable.)

Picture this as two long, skinny magnets sliding together with their
north poles facing each other. The magnets will resist touching, will
veer off and perhaps even spin around so one south pole can stick to the
other north pole. Now picture the magnets constrained in a groove so
they cannot spin around or veer off. What will happen? If one magnet

slides gently at the other, it will push the other one away and they will not make contact. But if the moving magnet is shot with great speed at the other magnet, it *will* make physical contact, after which it would bounce off, repelled by the matching magnetic pole. This is analogous to two protons approaching each other; they could make contact if they were going fast enough. Now imagine that the magnets have Velcro on them. If they come into contact, they will stick together. This Velcro force of attraction, which is very short range since it requires actual contact, will dominate the magnetic force of repulsion. If the magnets are pulled apart just enough to unhook the Velcro, the magnetic repul-

sion will take over and the magnets will move away from each other. The Velcro kicks in only when one magnet is shot with enough speed at the other to overcome the re-pulsion and make physi-cal contact.

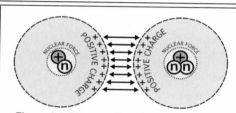

Figure 6.1. Diagram of two isotopes of hydrogen fusing. In order for the two atoms to fuse, the *gluons*, represented by the short arrows, have to overcome the mutual repulsion from the positive charges pushing them apart.

This Velcro attraction versus magnetic repul-sion resembles nuclear fusion. Particles that naturally repel each other can stick together if they make contact, as if they are covered in Velcro. The fusion process in nature is actually facilitated by particles called, appropriately, *gluons*, that have a powerful short-range attraction, just like Velcro. This fusion process is how the stars make the heavier elements. Two hydrogen atoms are "glued" together to make helium. Add another hydrogen and we get lithium. This picture is too simple however, and our Velcro analogy doesn't capture the full complexity of what is actually going on.

The biggest problem is carbon. And carbon happens to be the single most important atom for life, involved in so many life processes that the study of carbon and its many molecular arrangements is called *organic* chemistry. Carbon is, in fact, the *only* molecule around which we can build the incredibly complex molecules—sugars, acids, proteins—that make life possible. But the steps involved in the fusion process—the "gluing"—that goes from helium atoms up the staircase to carbon have problems. Some of the steps along the way are unstable.

TWINKLE, TWINKLE, LITTLE STAR

Clearly the stars knew how to build elements beyond iron,
even if the astrophysicists didn't.

TIMOTHY FERRIS

THE PRIMARY FUSION reaction in stars creates helium from hydrogen. If you are reading this book in natural sunlight, this is the reaction producing that light, 93 million miles away in the sun. There are a surprising number of steps to the process, which is shown in the insert section, figure N.

We start with four protons—two pairs—that have fused by slamming into each other in the intense heat of the star. Each of these proton-proton pairs is unstable, which means they can't remain for long in that state. They are immediately transformed by spontaneous reactions into a stable proton-neutron combination called deuterium. The nuclear reaction is driven by the aversion that two protons have for being stuck together when they find each other, literally, repulsive. The process works by converting one of the protons in the pair into a neutron and creating a positively charged particle called a positron in the process, to conserve the electrical charge. (The conservation of electrical charge is one of the most universal laws of nature and has never once been violated, as far as we know.) After the conversion process is complete, two deuterium nuclei fuse with another proton to create a proton-neutron-proton combination called helium-3. Two of these helium-3 combinations combine to create a highly unstable temporary conglomerate with four protons and two neutrons. This combination immediately kicks out two protons, leaving being a normal stable helium-4 nucleus, which is the typical form that would be found, for example, in a circus balloon. Helium is defined by the fact that it has two protons in its nucleus. Its nucleus can have either one or two neutrons in it.

The process of creating heavier elements would proceed smoothly from here if this stable helium atom could simply fuse with another proton to make lithium, and then this lithium atom would fuse with another proton to make element number four—beryllium—and so on, building the periodic table, one step at a time, like packing a snowball. Stars are full of protons buzzing about, crashing into everything, ready to fuse if they get a chance.

This simple procedure doesn't work because this particular lithium nucleus is unstable and splits apart immediately, before it has a chance to combine with anything to make the next element. Lithium needs

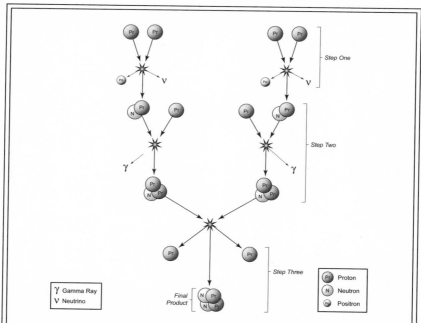

Figure 6.2. Four hydrogen nuclei are required to make one helium. To start, two pairs of protons separately form deuterium as shown in the first step of the diagram. The process involves a proton turning into a neutron and emitting a positively charged positron in the process, which carries away the positive charge of the proton. A particle called a neutrino is also emitted, which carries away a bit of surplus energy. In the next step, the two deuterium isotopes separately fuse with another proton to create the isotope helium-3. This releases some energy in the form of a gamma ray. In the last step, two of these deuterium isotopes combine into a big combination particle with four protons and two neutrons. This combination is unstable and immediately splits apart, kicking out two protons and leaving a stable helium-4 isotope behind, with two protons and two neutrons.

three or four neutrons in its nucleus to be stable. Adding a proton to helium creates an isotope of lithium that immediately disintegrates. So this path to even the second row on the periodic table is blocked. Another option would be for two helium atoms to fuse and create an isotope of beryllium with four protons and four neutrons. This, unfortunately, also doesn't work, since this nucleus also disintegrates almost immediately. A stable beryllium nucleus needs five neutrons, for reasons related to the details of nuclear physics.

So how do we get from helium to carbon if both the lithium path and the beryllium path are blocked? (We do, in fact, make both of these along the way, but in such tiny quantities that they are simply too rare to account for the great quantities of carbon that exists.) There is one other possibility, however, which avoids traveling either the lithium or beryllium path. What if *three* helium atoms fused together all at once? This is much more complicated than it sounds.

THE NOTORIOUS CARBON RESONANCE

*And so, with the help of God, Hoyle made heavy elements in this way,
but it was so complicated that nowadays neither Hoyle, nor God,
nor anybody else can figure out exactly how it was done.*

GEORGE GAMOW

THE STRANGEST EXPERIENCE of my long career as an amateur softball player and coach occurred at summer camp when I was a teenager. A strongly hit softball, destined to be a home run, struck a bird in flight and killed it. The ball and the bird dropped into shallow center field, cancelling the home run. The probability of this event was so low that it would be hard to even calculate; the batter who killed the bird held celebrity status for the rest of the week, despite some sympathy for the hapless bird. Now imagine an even more improbable event. Suppose there was a second softball game on a nearby field and a very long home run from that game had struck the same bird at the same time. This story would be simply unbelievable, and were I to offer it as a true story, you would be rightly skeptical. For a bird in flight and two soaring softballs to be in the same place at the same time is too improbable to imagine, unless someone engineered the whole thing as a stunt.

In the same way, the fusion of any three atoms is a highly improbable event. The fusion of two atoms is also low probability and occurs with regularity only because there are so many atoms buzzing about that they will occasionally smash into each other, like cars on the highway. Three atoms smashing into each other at exactly the same time, while not impossible, will not occur frequently enough to be an important part of any process.

In the case of helium, there are two ways for three atoms to get together: (1) two helium atoms could form a beryllium and a third helium fuse with the combination before it disintegrated in a split second, or (2) the three atoms could fuse together all at once into a stable carbon. If you work out the probabilities, neither of these processes occurs with enough probability to account for the carbon. So how did the star produce all the carbon (see insert figure N)?

Enter Fred Hoyle, a brash British physicist making a grand entrance with a grand idea. Hoyle felt in his bones that there was something missing in the explanation. The bottlenecks described previously were too serious to permit the production of carbon in the large quantities in which it was found. So he went looking for some hidden assistance to the process.

Hoyle understood that the key to getting things to happen in nature—or in the immigration office described at the beginning of this chapter—was to match up the energies. If you provide *exactly* the energy that is needed to make a new arrangement, nature was much happier than if you provided too much, just like the bureaucrat in the immigration office. In most natural processes there is a surplus of energy, and nature has to find some way to unload it. In figure 6.2 the gamma ray is emitted to carry off excess energy when the second step of the fusion reaction occurs.

In a manner of speaking, the system has to perform a quick energy audit, determine the amount of surplus energy, weigh the options for getting rid the surplus, choose one and then create and emit the radiation or particle(s) necessary to carry away the surplus energy. If the energy was perfectly matched, this step would not be needed and the fusion reaction would be more efficient—proceed much faster. So Hoyle calculated the exact energy that three helium atoms would bring to the table, so to speak, if they were to fuse. The amount was, unfortunately, *higher* than that possessed by the carbon atom, so the process would be slowed down by the need to emit this extra energy. But there was one other possibility.

Nuclei, atoms and molecules all have multiple energy states. There is a stable lowest energy state, but there are also higher energy states that the particles can be in sometimes, usually just for a brief moment. What if carbon had a slightly higher energy state that was exactly equal to the energy of the three helium atoms? In this case the reaction would be much more efficient, making up for the low probability of the three helium atoms getting together.

Physicists knew nothing about any such higher energy state helping along the fusion of carbon. Hoyle thus had to convince some experimental physicists to do some new and complicated experiments to find this higher energy state, called the *carbon resonance*. Physicists, in fact, knew little about the higher energy states, or resonances, of nuclei in general, so Hoyle's proposal—to continue our softball analogy—came out of left field.

In 1951, three years after proposing the steady state theory—an even more left field idea—the still unknown Hoyle showed up at the California Institute of Technology, where some physicists worked with the specialized apparatus that would possibly find the carbon resonance. Willy Fowler, who would go on to win a Nobel Prize, and his colleagues were incredulous that this cocky unsung Brit with a working-class accent was pressing them to perform this complex experiment to find something that, if it existed, should have been discovered already. Eventually they were persuaded and began the long process of reconfiguring their equipment to look more closely at carbon. Amazingly, they found a previously unknown energy level in carbon, one that made it possible for three helium atoms to combine without getting frustrated by energy mismatches. It was yet another example of the remarkable power of prediction in science.

It was now clear there was no carbon bottleneck. The fusion process had no barriers preventing it from moving productively forward on the periodic table, creating oxygen, neon, magnesium and on to iron.

WHY DOES IT MATTER?

*The origin of the universe and of the constants of nature
is a mystery, and may forever remain so.*

Timothy Ferris

THE ENERGY LEVEL known as the carbon resonance has to be exactly right—no margin for error. If the resonance was a fraction of a percent lower or higher, the process would not work and the carbon bottleneck would prevent the formation of the chemicals necessary for life. Life in the universe hangs on this thread.

The carbon resonance depends in an intricate way on the precise details of the laws of physics—laws of physics that preceded the creation of the universe. In particular it depends on the strength of the force—the Velcro—that holds protons and neutrons together in the nucleus. Where does this force come from? Is there any explanation for why it has the particular strength that it does? The answer is no—the Velcro force—actually the *strong nuclear force*—is just one of those features of the universe that are what they are. Somehow, when the universe was born, this particular nuclear force had exactly the right value to empower carbon production—a process that would get started only billions of years later when the stars had formed and fusion reactions were running full steam ahead.

This discovery, understandably, impressed Hoyle deeply. It also impressed his critics. "It looks like a put-up job," Hoyle suggested, tongue in cheek. The precision of the numbers suggested to him that a "superintellect has monkeyed with physics," an interesting speculation for an atheist.

Hoyle's discovery of the carbon resonance reveals in a most interesting way the deep relationship between the laws of the physics—not biology—and the habitability of the universe. In ways that would not have been apparent a century ago, we now understand that the laws of physics have to be exactly as they are or the universe will not be habitable. And the carbon resonance is far from the only example. All the other laws have their own interesting relationship to the habitability of the universe.

We now understand that life, despite being rare in the universe—most planets and all stars are sterile—is interwoven with both the laws of physics that existed when the universe began and the detailed way that the universe evolved under the influence of those laws.

Consider gravity. When the big bang occurred gravity worked against the outward expansion of all the matter in the universe. If gravity were the only phenomenon of relevance at the time, the universe would have collapsed back in on itself. Instead a delicate balance existed between the energy of the expansion, working to separate everything, and gravity, working to gather

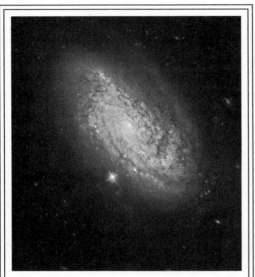

Figure 6.3. This is galaxy NGC 3021. Galaxies illustrate the balance between gravitational forces of attraction and other forces working against gravity. Galaxies rotate, which creates an outward centrifugal force. Changing the strength of gravity will change the actual size of the galaxy. (NASA, ESA, and A. Riess [STScI/JHU]/Wikimedia Commons)

it back into one big black hole. Computer simulations have allowed physicists to construct models of the universe where gravity differs slightly from its present strength. The results are provocative.

If gravity were a tiny bit stronger, it would have gathered the matter of the universe more effectively after the big bang with the result that all the matter would collapse back into a single massive black hole, with no possibility of life. On the other hand, if gravity were a tiny bit weaker, the initial distribution of atoms in the early universe would spread out so quickly that they would be dispersed before they had a chance to collect into stars.

As with the nuclear forces that make fusion work, we have no explanation for why gravity has the strength that it does. All we know is that gravity has to have the particular strength that it has or the universe would not be habitable. To emphasize the pure inexplicability of the detailed features of gravity, we refer to it as a *brute fact* of the universe. We simply have to accept it as true without explanation.

Scientists, not surprisingly, don't like brute facts. For important features of our universe to be utterly inexplicable is as disturbing as the sound of fingernails dragging on a chalkboard. Scientists who work on fundamental physics search hopefully for a theory that will one day explain why our universe is built on this particular set of brute facts. But for now those brute facts just hover in front of us, dragging their fingernails on the chalkboard, taunting us to try to explain them.

Unfortunately for those who can't stand the sound of fingernails on chalkboards, there are many brute facts. One especially important one relates to the mass of the particles in the universe. The ratio of the mass of the proton to the electron is the uninteresting number 1836.1526675. The electron is much lighter than the proton. The ratio of the mass of the neutron to the proton is 1.00137841870, which is very close to 1 and also uninteresting. The neutron is just a fraction of a percent heavier. These are just bland numbers of the sort that frighten teenagers and make them not want to major in physics. But these numbers are quite interesting when we inquire into their significance.

Because the neutron is slightly *heavier* than the proton, the laws of physics permit isolated neutrons to convert spontaneously—*decay*—into protons, with an electron emitted to balance the electrical charge. (Neutrons embedded in a nucleus, fused to protons and other neutrons, are stable and unlikely to decay.) The decay of neutrons is not a big deal though, and losing them has no consequences for life. On the other hand, if the neutron were lighter by a fraction of just 1 percent, it would be possible for isolated protons to decay into neutrons. (Particles can only decay into lighter particles because of conservation of energy.) Since for much of the history of the universe protons have existed in isolation, this would be disastrous for life. Most or all of them would be gone now, and all the critically important atoms needed for life would not exist.

Why do these particles have the masses they do? Once again, these are simply brute facts of the universe. There is no explanation, but they have to be as they are or we would not be here.

TWIDDLING THE COSMIC KNOBS

If we are allowed to think of God in anthropomorphic terms,
we would have to say, "Good planning."

OWEN GINGERICH

THESE EXAMPLES CAN be multiplied further but there is no need. Just as you don't have to note the price of everything in the grocery store to see that prices are going up, so you don't have to examine every detail of the physical universe to see how remarkably designed it appears for life.

Paul Davies, one of the more thoughtful physicists working on this interesting problem, won the Templeton Prize for Progress in Religion in 1995. Davies, while not a traditional religious believer, approaches these questions honestly and openly, following C. S. Lewis's admonition to "follow the argument where it leads." Davies uses the analogy of a "Designer Machine" to describe what is going on.

The Designer Machine has knobs that must be set to precise values if the universe is to be habitable. If one knob is set on the wrong value, then the universe will never have life in it. Davies estimates that there are some twenty knobs associated with the details of the universe that have to be set in order for the laws of physics to start working. The masses of the particles that we looked at briefly above are examples of this. The charge on the electron and the strength of the strong nuclear—Velcro—force are others.

Ten additional knobs related to cosmology have to be set to the correct values. The expansion rate of the universe is one example. A universe expanding too fast will disperse all its matter before any stars can form. A universe expanding too slowly will have all its matter gathered almost immediately back into a black hole. A universe with a life-supporting collection of long-lived stars has to be expanding at exactly the right rate.[2]

Not all of the knobs on the Designer Machine have to be set with the same precision. And some of them may not be independent of each other. It could be that setting one knob, in some way we don't understand, automatically sets the value of another knob. We don't know enough to figure out exactly what is going on. Some knobs can be off by the better part of a percent, some even more. Some have to be set with astonishing precision.

The knobs on the Designer Machine relate to the universe as a whole. They specify what sort of universe can have stars with planets orbiting them—a Goldilocks universe. In a way that we have gradually come to understand over the course of the last century, physics forms an amazing foundation for biology. Countless settings on the Designer Machine create a universe with physics but no biology. And so few settings— perhaps just one—create a universe that can accommodate life (see insert figure O).

This state of affairs cries out for explanation. Attempts to explain it abound. Is life just a huge fluke? Have we hit the "cosmic jackpot," as Paul Davies titled his book? Or are we peering into "the mind of God," as he titled an earlier book?

Freeman Dyson, one of the greatest and most thoughtful physicists of the twentieth century, reflected on this question in his autobiography, *Disturbing the Universe*. Dyson was a colleague of Albert Einstein, Robert Oppenheimer and other luminaries

Figure 6.4. Freeman Dyson, who made the provocative statement, "The universe in some sense must have known we were coming." Dyson won the Templeton Prize for Progress in Religion in 2000. (Jacob Appelbaum/Wikimedia Commons)

at the Princeton Institute for Advanced Study, a think tank where the brightest minds receive a generous salary to simply think. Dyson made his mark in physics by answering some of the deeper questions about the nature of quantum mechanics. His stature in the scientific community, like that of Einstein, freed him from the need to be intellectually cautious, and he developed a reputation for acknowledging the deeper mysteries of our existence. Never a conventional religious believer, Dyson did, nonetheless, believe that there was more to the universe than the raw material of physics. In particular he marveled at how the features of the universe present at its birth—the laws of physics and the details of the big bang—synergistically worked to move the universe steadily in the direction of habitability. A universe that might have seemed at first to be going nowhere in particular turned out to be heading steadily in our direction. "The more I examine the universe and study the details of its architecture," Dyson wrote in *Disturbing the Universe*, "the more evidence I find that the universe in some sense must have known we were coming."[3]

INTERLUDE:
CROSSING THE
UNCERTAIN BRIDGE

Can We Get from Science to Religion?

There are few familiar words that can describe the universe as a whole. Those who study the universe use physics and mathematics, but what are their equations about?

JOEL PRIMACK AND NANCY ELLEN ABRAMS

SCIENCE, AS DISCUSSED IN PART ONE of this book, has discovered much about the universe. The scientific enterprise provides amazing insights into the natural world, and I have argued that those insights are reliable, steadily improving and most likely true. Caution and humility are in order, nonetheless, because science is a finite human enterprise with all the limitations that entails.

Skeptics of various sorts, from young-earth creationists to agnostic postmodern literary critics, sometimes dispute the claims of science, pointing to past scientific ideas that have been overturned or areas of present controversy. The settled and secure science of today, suggest these critics, may pass into history, joining the settled and secure science of yesterday in the graveyard of wrong ideas.

There is some truth to this caution, but it really should be nothing more than a caution, like a seatbelt put on with no expectation of needing

Figures I.1-4. Infamous skeptics. Kelvin, Einstein, Hoyle and Dyson were all great physicists who made important contributions to physics. Yet each of them strongly opposed a central idea accepted by his peers. Kelvin rejected the age of the earth being determined by the geologists; Einstein never accepted that quantum mechanics contained genuine randomness; Hoyle never accepted the big bang theory; and Dyson, still alive at the time of this writing, does not accept that global warming is a threat to the welfare of the planet. (Lord Kelvin: Wikimedia Commons; Albert Einstein: Wikimedia Commons; Freeman Dyson: Lumidek/ Wikimedia Commons; Fred Hoyle: Donald D. Clayton/AIP Emilio Segre Visual Archives, Clayton Collection)

it. During every major, and even minor, transition in science there are people who hold to traditional views; there are examples of tenacious and irrational loyalty to the status quo. There are many celebrity skeptics. Einstein wouldn't accept quantum mechanics. Lord Kelvin wouldn't accept the emerging evidence for an ancient earth at the end of the nineteenth century. Galileo wouldn't accept Kepler's calculations that showed that the planetary orbits were elliptical rather than circular. Fred Hoyle, as we saw earlier, wouldn't accept the evidence for the big bang and developed a theory to oppose it.

Those eager to reject the claims of science invoke these anecdotes as if they are typical. If we don't like the fact that science has determined the age of the earth to be billions of years old, we cling to the hope that this conclusion, like the once-secure claim that the earth is stationary, will soon give way to a new and more congenial understanding. After all, for two thousand years educated leaders insisted that a mountain of evidence pointed to the earth being stationary and at the center of the universe. And now no scientist believes that. Similarly, Newton's ideas were supplanted by those of Einstein. Quantum mechanics, black holes, multiple universes and string theory have blown everyone's mind at some point over the past century. Is there any good reason to believe that the new ideas of tomorrow will be different and perhaps more appealing than the ideas of today?

The answer, in a nutshell, is no.

IS SCIENCE CONSTANTLY CHANGING ITS MIND?

Remember first of all that science has changed and has gone through many transformations. The assured results of modern science today may very well not be the assured results of modern science tomorrow. And, I can promise you, are not the assured results of science yesterday.

AL MOHLER

THE IDEA THAT science constantly changes is largely fiction, based on our lopsided familiarity with scientific revolutions and lack of awareness of ongoing ordinary science. The typical scientific advance—the sort that is presented in almost every one of the thousands of scientific papers published each year—is one that *extends, encompasses* and *absorbs* rather than *refutes* old understandings. Only rarely do new ideas require that old ideas be discarded.

Even truly revolutionary ideas are often compatible with many previous ideas. Consider Copernicus's ideas—the gold standard for scientific revolutions. His new model for the solar system included the all-important but long-established ideas that the planets were different than the stars, that the planets all had their own orbits, that the stars maintained predictable patterns, and, of course, that the earth was round. We overlook the significance of this because science often establishes its conclusions with such clarity that they seem trivial, and thus their enduring character seems inconsequential. But the discovery and measurement of the shape and size of the earth, for example, was an amazing achievement. Similarly, Newton's ideas have not been discarded; they simply have been shown to have a restricted domain of application. When I teach mechanics to engineering students, I use a textbook based entirely on Newton's laws of motion. If Newton's own treatment wasn't so opaque, we could still be using his book from the seventeenth century. The revolution that "toppled Newton" was the discovery of certain extreme situations where his theory did not work. It was not the discovery that his ideas were wrong in any simple sense. NASA still launches space shuttles and puts satellites into orbit using Newton's laws, which work perfectly for those situations. The repeated discovery of new planets—as exciting as it was at the time—simply expanded the domain of application of Newton's theory of gravity.

The application of scientific ideas to technological devices provides another reason for being comfortable with science. Scientific insights that have given rise to technologies like computers, cell phones and lasers have a certain pragmatic credibility and are unlikely to be supplanted. If those ideas were not true, then building devices based on them would be impossible. Almost all the physics of the first half of the twentieth century is validated every time your computer powers up. No matter what you think about the strangeness of quantum mechanics, the devices based on it work.

The prudent approach to science is to accept its central ideas as good descriptions of reality, developed by scientists, working with integrity, who are motivated to find out how the created world functions. The central ideas in any scientific field—whether it be cosmology or medicine—have been hammered out by a community of well-informed and highly skeptical scientists. To achieve consensus with such a group is no simple task.

Appreciating the consensus character of science is crucial to navigating scientific controversies like those that swirl about global warming, the big bang or biological evolution. The central ideas of science are *never* based entirely on the work of a few scientists. While certain great scientists like Darwin or Einstein may provide the initial flash of genius, the idea flows from the margins of science into a much larger world until thousands of skeptical specialists are thinking hard about it. Many of those specialists are looking for an ingenious flaw in the theory, just as Einstein tried heroically to come up with a good reason to reject quantum mechanics. The simple fact that quantum mechanics survived a quarter century of assault by Einstein should convince us that the theory must be reliable. But this same fire refines every idea in science. The moment a new idea appears in the scientific literature, critics spring into action, motivated by everything from self-defense to curiosity to an enthusiasm for knowledge to a desire to be famous.

As I write these words a great controversy swirls about a recent paper in *Science* claiming that a bacterium has arsenic instead of phosphorous in its DNA. This is a startling claim with many implications for understanding life. Leading biologist Jerry Coyne blogged on June 5, 2011, expressing his doubts that the arsenic claim will survive the scrutiny it is getting. He notes that as soon as the research came out "a lot of critics began to weigh in with serious questions about the paper's results, with some researchers declaring it fatally flawed. Bloggers, scientists, and journalists . . . all noted problems with the paper."[1] Coyne's description is typical of how science works and how incredibly hard it is for a radically new idea to gain support.

New ideas from the fringes lobbying to get into the scientific conversation can be taken seriously but not uncritically. They may be the explanations of tomorrow, or they may pass like the "cold fusion" claims from the 1980s, which I suspect you have never heard about, despite making a great stir at the time. There is presently a lot of excitement about multiple universes. I am skeptical that these ideas will endure, but the right people are proposing them in the right way, so we have to take them seriously. We should not dig in our heels, as some did against the ideas of Galileo, and cut off discussion. These ideas may withstand the scrutiny they are receiving now. For truly controversial ideas, we should look closely at who is saying what, and why they are saying it. Great scientists, from Newton to Einstein to Dyson will often end their illustrious careers exploring oddball ideas that would sink the careers of lesser scientists.

And of course one should always be skeptical of the way that zealous scientific crusaders misuse science to make some larger point that has nothing to do with science. Atheists claiming that Darwin forces us to abandon belief in God are the best example of this.

The most difficult part of science for an outsider to navigate is scientific controversy. Many ideas in science—and many other fields, for that matter—are opposed by dissenters. Often these dissenters have Ph.D.s and are well-credentialed. They may have written books and hold appointments at respected universities. How are we to know if the controversial idea held by the dissenter, and being opposed by people too invested in the status quo, is the new science of tomorrow? Is it possible that the status quo is on its way to becoming the science of yesterday, and its champions are just the faithful few who just can't let go? If two scholars holding opposite ideas are pitted against each other and both have comparable credentials, what do you do?

Consider the case of Francis Collins and Michael Behe, who are both Christians, although that is not technically important for the point I am making. Collins is a well-respected geneticist who headed the Human Genome Project and, as of right now, directs the National Institutes of Health, overseeing the largest biomedical research budget in the world. He has written several books, including the bestseller *The Language of*

God: A Scientist Presents Evidence for Belief. In 2011 he and I coauthored *The Language of Faith and Science: Straight Answers to Genuine Questions.* In both of these books, in his public presentations and in his many research papers he affirms the theory of evolution and the adequacy of that theory to explain the development of life on this planet.

Michael Behe is a fully credentialed biochemist tenured at Lehigh University, a respected research institution. He has published more than one hundred research papers and has written two bestselling books: *Darwin's Black Box: The Biochemical Challenge to Evolution* and *The Edge of Evolution: The Search for the Limits of Darwinism.* In both of these books he denies the theory of evolution by unguided mechanisms like natural selection, claiming it cannot account for the development of life on this planet. He does, however, accept the common ancestry of all life.

Who is right—Collins or Behe? And how do we decide? Almost all the controversies about science within the evangelical world—and else-

Figures I.5-6. Collins is an evangelical Christian and Behe is Roman Catholic. Both have Ph.D.s and both are recognized scholars. Yet they are diametrically opposed on what the evidence from genetics is telling us about evolution. Collins's book presents mainstream science, in agreement with the scientific community. Behe's book presents arguments that few other scientists take seriously.

where—come down to this sort of situation—multiple experts, often impressively credentialed, but with opposing views. Behe and Collins both claim to speak for science. I want to suggest that, despite the apparent symmetry of the two sides in this case, that Collins should clearly be preferred over Behe.

Collins promotes scientific ideas that are shared by tens of thousands of other credentialed scientists. The pages of leading science magazines discuss those ideas. Scientific meetings put those ideas on their programs. Grants are awarded to study those ideas. Biotechnology companies research new products based on those ideas. Some pharmaceutical companies even have products for sale based on those ideas. In contrast, Behe's ideas are shared by a tiny number of scientists, and most of them are less credentialed than he is. Collins's group of colleagues is hundreds, perhaps thousands of times larger than Behe's. The ideas about intelligent design promoted by Behe are almost nonexistent in the scientific literature. Some of the ideas, in fact, have *never* been written up and submitted to a science journal. They appear only in his popular books. Behe's ideas are not discussed at scientific meetings but only at gatherings of like-minded Christians who are often suspicious of science. They are published primarily in books that are not peer reviewed in the way that scientific research is peer reviewed before it is published. No grants are being awarded to study these ideas and no companies are interested in creating products based on them.

Behe represents a common phenomenon in American culture—the heroic but lonely outsider defending a view rejected by the majority. He is like the handful of climate scientists who deny global warming. Or the champions of the existence of actual cases of alien abduction, some of whom are credible scholars.

This is not to say, of course, that Behe is wrong. Holding a minority view is not the same as being wrong. Most of the major ideas in science were once minority viewpoints embraced by a few renegade thinkers marching to their own drummer. But it does mean that Behe's views cannot properly be called scientific, in the normal definition of that term. Science works by achieving *consensus*, and only those ideas that have secured the allegiance of the scientific community can legitimately be called scientific. Other ideas might be up-and-coming; they might even be true. But they cannot be considered genuinely scientific ideas until they have persuaded the majority of scientists. And scientists, by temperament, are hard to persuade.

SO HOW DOES SCIENCE WORK?

Our culture has changed vastly since the mid-twentieth century. Science has become much less cool, scientists have ceased to be role models and kids aren't rushing home anymore to fire rockets from their backyards.

CHRIS MOONEY AND SHERIL KIRSHENBAUM

THE CLAIM THAT science works by consensus raises the important question of what sort of ideas are most likely to create this consensus. How, exactly, do scientists all arrive at the same conclusion? If, for example, consensus is achieved through bribery, threats, blind allegiance to celebrity scientists or fear of losing one's job, then we can hardly fault the skeptic for being unimpressed with consensus endorsements. The question of the nature of science—its definitions, boundaries, methods and criteria for evaluation—is elusive and complicated. For as long as impressive explanations for natural phenomena have been generated there has been a companion activity analyzing the process. It is called the philosophy of science.

Francis Bacon, born shortly after Copernicus died, was the first in a long line of armchair scientific quarterbacks. Often referred to as the "father of the scientific method," Bacon argued forcefully that natural science should work *inductively*, reasoning from facts to conclusions, rather than *syllogistically*, as the tradition deriving from Aristotle and Plato emphasized.[2] Induction works by looking at *specifics*—"all the rocks in the pail I collected on this beach are white"—and moving to generalizations—"Therefore, all the rocks on this beach are white." Only by starting with clear and uncontroversial facts can we be sure we were not letting our assumptions, prejudices and imaginations run away with us. The price we paid for this objectivity was a lack of absolute certainty. Being inductive, Baconian science was probabilistic, not absolute. But if the data is adequate the probabilities can approach certainty, so this was not a serious problem. (Who really doubts the sun will come up tomorrow, even though the evidence, being based on a finite number of observations of sunrises, is not absolute?) For Bacon, science was *defined* by induction. If your conclusions were carefully and inductively derived, they could be described as scientific.

Bacon's explanation, and most of those that followed, trying to improve on his work, were inadequate on many fronts. Bacon's "facts" were sometimes not so simple and often needed a theory or some larger framework to makes sense of them. A Baconian "fact" might be the position of a star or planet overhead. But in order to state exactly where that planet is, one has to do a lot of theoretical work, noting the position of the earth, the distance to the star or planet and so on. Aristotle and Galileo, for example, could agree on the observational fact of the position of a wandering star in the sky. But they held different views of the structure of the solar system, so they would calculate very different actual locations for the wandering star. A star does not a have a tag hanging from one the five points, listing its position. Without this larger framework, the *simple* observation of the star can't be understood.

Figure I.7. Francis Bacon (1561-1626) has been called the father of empiricism. At a time when scientific practice was still undefined, he emphasized observation and induction as the proper approach to understanding nature. (Wikimedia Commons)

Alternative philosophies of science—and there were many proposed over the centuries that followed Bacon—did little better. In the final analysis it is impossible to develop criteria that we can use to analyze a particular idea at a particular time and determine whether or not it is scientific. But all is not lost. In fact, there is an entirely different way of framing this problem of the criteria for good science.

Instead of looking at a particular idea—theory, law, hypothesis—at a *moment* in time, we look at it over a *period* of time. If the idea consistently *generates new knowledge* and its explanatory power *grows*, then we become convinced it must be true. If the idea survives challenges, we pass approval on it and our confidence grows. We thus look at what the idea *does* rather than what it *is*.

Take Newton's theory of gravity. It was developed using only the earth-moon system as its basis. If we were to look at Newton's theory at that moment in time, it would be difficult to determine just how scientific it was. A skeptic might counter that the theory was fudged to match that particular system and the formula was not really "universal." Determining that Newton's theory was better "science" when it first appeared than the alternative view—"all celestial bodies orbit in circles under the influence of innate driving forces"—would have been challenging. But over the next few years Newton's theory would explain the orbits of Venus, Mars and Jupiter. It would explain the moons about Jupiter. It would withstand challenges from the wobbly orbits of Saturn and Uranus, and actually predict the existence of two planets. Newton's theory of gravity proved to be a reliable guide to new knowledge, and those that accepted it became steadily more confident in its power. The idea itself did not change. The law of universal gravity was exactly the same in 1900 as it was in 1700. And yet, by 1900 everyone was convinced it was true, unlike 1700 when it was still battling competitors.

In contrast the prevailing ideas inherited from Greece, and some challenges from French scientists like Descartes, proved sterile.

During the period of transition from the traditional Aristotelian view to the new Copernican view, both systems competed. The consensus that developed in favor of Copernicus was not the result of a static comparison of the two views to see which was more "scientific." There were decades when such a comparison would have been pointless. Galileo, despite his heroic efforts, could find no convincing argument to bring people around to his view. Rather, as astronomers worked with both systems over decades, they found the Copernican system to fit better with what they were trying to do. It was, for example, easier to use. This allowed more time for calculations—incredibly time-consuming in the days before calculators—and that brought more people around to its simplicity. Its simplicity gave it a performance edge not possessed by its competitor. Simplicity, though, is not really quantifiable. Gradually people are drawn to the new system because it works better for what they are trying to do. But this was a judgment made by many scientists over time, not a static comparison.

In this more dynamic view, attention is focused on what the ideas *do* rather than the logical structure of the ideas themselves or whether the ideas have been established by specific observations. By analogy this would be like evaluating medicine in terms of its *effects* rather than its chemical *composition*. Imagine you have a brand new chemical to cure strep throat. The chemical will have a formula—a molecular structure—that locates its various atoms with respect to each other. Is this molecule a cure for strep throat? Is it a medicine at all? What sort of definition would be appropriate to decide if the molecule is medicinal?

Figure I.8. René Descartes (1596-1650) developed an alternative explanation for the motion of the planets. This view was popular enough that Newton took great care to explain why his theory of gravity was superior. Descartes explained planetary motions in terms of vortices—whirlpools of invisible material in space that carried the planets around. Some seventeenth-century thinkers pre-ferred this model, but it failed to generate new insights and gradually disappeared from the conversation. It did not disappear by being refuted so much as by failing to provide anything useful to scientists working on this problem. (Used by permission. ©Georgios Kollidas/depositphotos)

Would it not simply make more sense to suspend judgment on questions of molecular structure and see if the medicine actually works? If it cures strep throat consistently, we conclude that it is medicine, regardless of its structure. We could even conclude—as is the case with some medicines—that we have no idea how it works; we simply know that it does.

Ideas that prove reliable guides to new truth are like medicines that work—their proof is in their pudding. This is the best way to think about ideas that claim to be scientific. Does working with them generate new knowledge about the world? Do the ideas easily incorporate new information, as it is discovered? Do the ideas make startling and remarkable predictions that can be confirmed?

In the final analysis there is no way to draw a clean boundary between science and nonscience. Scientists agree that astronomy is a science and astrology is not. Dowsing, the process of finding underground water by walking around with a twig that points to the underground water when standing above it, is not science. It is nonsense. People who do it or hire it out to dowsers are wasting their time and money. Solid-state physics, in contrast, is clearly a science and those researchers trying to make better touchpads for tablets and smart phones are certainly doing science. Discussion about multiple universes, however, is more ambiguous. It is certainly more scientific than astrology or dowsing—which isn't saying much—but not as scientific as solid-state physics. It could *become* mainstream science at some point, but it is not there yet. Multiverse enthusiasts are working hard to find some empirical evidence for the idea, which is exactly what they should be doing. And in late 2010 some tentative evidence was discovered, but its speculative character is not entirely convincing.[3]

There is also no way to identify a time when an idea makes the transition from speculation to science. Eddington's measurement of the bending of starlight carried Einstein's theory of general relativity across the threshold into science, in the opinion of many. George Lemaître's initial proposal for the big bang, however, was derided by his critics as being a religious—rather than scientific—idea, despite being based on both general relativity and Hubble's observation of the recession of the galaxies. Gamow's prediction of leftover radiation from the big bang indicates that Lemaître's idea was at least in the scientific ballpark, even though no way existed to detect that radiation. The discovery of the universal background radiation in 1965, however, certainly established the genuinely scientific character of the big bang as well as its truth. But there is no way to find a line of demarcation with *real* science on one side and *aspiring* science on the other.

The impossibility of finding clear bright lines dividing science from nonscience or good science from bad science or even true scientific ideas from refuted scientific ideas is not a serious problem. It does not, for example, mean that any and all ideas are worthy of consideration just because we can't say with absolute clarity where those ideas lie on the meandering and poorly mapped path running from nonscience to science. All it means is that science, however we think about it, must be understood in terms of a *spectrum*, like so many other things. Nobody is troubled about the distinction between night and day just because there is no clear line at sunrise and sunset, when one passes into the other. Rich and poor are not mysteriously the same because a continuous and broad range of middle-class positions separates them, with no gap. Fast and slow, old and young, stupid and smart and most other aspects of the world we inhabit are not neatly compartmentalized into two boxes in such a way that not being in one box automatically puts one in the other. The world, as we learn growing up, is often arrayed in shades of gray, not black and white.

All of these cautions and ambiguities highlight the important role played by scientific experience and the collective wisdom of the community of scientists. The need for so many judgment calls cautions us against paying too much attention to fringe or minority viewpoints. Enough ambiguity always exists that some small group may be outside the consensus for reasons that make sense to them. But the safest and most secure notions are those that that have been scrutinized and embraced by the majority in the community. Scientists are cranky and argumentative. They march to their own drummers along their own idiosyncratic roads. So when these roads converge to the same address, we can be quite comfortable with that destination.

The scientific community has developed various techniques, both formal and informal, over the past few centuries to facilitate this convergence—to assure that generally accepted results are as reliable as possible.

1. For starters, *peer review* assures that the most knowledgeable experts will have a look at ideas before they are published. Peer review is often contentious, and editors are likely to send a study making a controversial claim to a reviewer inclined to be hostile to such ideas. Peer review is *not* a cabal of insiders keeping out new ideas, as critics charge. Every single scientific paper contains a new idea, and countless radical ideas have made their way successfully into science. Scientific journals will even publish papers with opposing viewpoints, if the ideas have merit. The big bang and steady-state cosmologies were incompatible but were both in the scientific literature at the same time for several years.

2. *Repeatability* assures that other researchers, with slightly—or even significantly—different experimental setups can duplicate the ideas. If your magical, new, I-could-win-a-Nobel-Prize particle discovered in Boston doesn't show up when the physicists in Moscow duplicate your experiment, then too bad for your new particle and your Nobel Prize. A great many ideas have fallen by the wayside because they could not be repeated. Such failures often lead to other discoveries but the demand for repeatability provides an invaluable reality check. Extraordinary and unexpected claims are likely to get the strongest scrutiny and anyone who is skeptical of a new idea can simply repeat the experiment if he or she wants to challenge it.

3. The vast network of interlocking ideas already in place provides a powerful collective intuition about what sorts of new ideas are most unusual and in need of careful inspection. Data suggesting that watching reality TV cures the common cold, no matter how impressive, will receive aggressive and heightened scrutiny because such a claim is so far outside the accepted network of scientific ideas. A colleague's data suggesting that chicken soup cures the common cold will not be met with the same opposition. Chicken soup is a complex mixture of ingredients that could conceivably help with the common cold.

Ideas championed by small groups of outsiders—like Michael Behe and other antievolutionists at the Discovery Institute—should be challenged with a very reasonable question: If these ideas are so compelling, why don't more knowledgeable scientists accept them? And if these ideas are viable, why are their champions not making their case within the scientific community?

The response to these questions takes one of two forms: Those who *agree* with the ideas being proposed by the outsiders accuse the scientific community of willful ignorance and irrational stubbornness. They cherry-pick history for a few examples where scientists were too dismissive of new ideas, too confident about current ones or too gullible in the acceptance of things they wished were true. They then present those examples—the long tenure of geocentrism before Copernicus, the fake Piltdown Man fossils that were mistakenly hailed as a critical missing link, the Miller-Urey experiment ballyhooed as providing evidence for the origins of life when all it showed was how to get amino acids—as if they were *typical* examples of how unreliable or exaggerated the "assured results of science" really are. On the other hand, those who *disagree* with the ideas being posed by the outsiders simply note that these ideas come from outside the scientific community and assume that if they had any merit, they would be inside the community already.

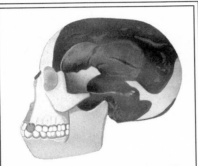

Figure I.9. The infamous fossil of Piltdown Man was long hailed as an important "missing link" in human evolution. Pictured in many textbooks and widely accepted, it was eventually discovered to be not just an error but a hoax. Someone planted the bones where an eager paleontologist would find them and created an embarrassing misperception. Paleontologists, not critics of evolution, discovered and exposed the hoax. (J. Arthur Thomson/Wikimedia Commons)

There is no simple way, of course, to know when an idea is past its prime and in need of discarding. Such ideas do not develop mold around the edges like cheese past its prime. In the final analysis evaluating the exact strength and staying power of a theory at a particular moment in time is impossible. The best plan—the one that has the strongest history of being prudent—is to trust the generally accepted picture of science. After all, that is what sensible people do in the doctor's office. Few of us prefer medical treatments promoted by eccentric outsiders.

SO WHAT DOES SCIENCE TELL US?

As children tremble and fear everything in the blind darkness,
so we in the light sometimes fear what is no more to be feared
than the things children in the dark hold in terror.

LUCRETIUS

THE PRECEDING COMMENTS are not intended to trumpet the in-
fallibility of science. Few scientists, at least in their calmer moments,
make claims that science is infallible. I simply want to take the central
and settled ideas of science seriously and ask what those ideas tell us
about the world.

In the rest of this book I want to explore some ideas that rest on this
foundation of science. I think science is telling us something about the
world that is *encouraging* rather than *threatening* to a worldview that
embraces God as the foundation of reality. Most of all I want to discuss ways that currently accepted scientific ideas can be embraced by
Christians as encouragements to faith, rather than challenges. If
Christians spend their energies in a futile search for an alternate science—which is what so many are doing now—rather than a careful
reflection on the science of the scientific community, they will miss
some wonderful insights.

Part one of this book has laid out the case that the universe is wonderful, surprising and provocatively friendly to life. The laws of physics
appear to have been "monkeyed with by a superintellect" to paraphrase
Fred Hoyle. Hoyle, however, offers an interesting caution to how we
evaluate the apparent design of the universe. Despite his role in discovering design and his intuition about a "superintellect" behind the patterns of nature, Hoyle remained an agnostic to the end of his life. He
was not convinced by his own discoveries. In the same way, Freeman
Dyson sees an unfolding purpose in a universe that "knew we were
coming," and yet he did not conclude that God was responsible—only
that there is something interesting going on. The evidence that seems
so apparent to religious believers is strangely unpersuasive to those
without prior beliefs.

WHAT IS THE POINT?

*If the purpose of the Cosmos is to evolve mind, we must regard it as
rather incompetent in having produced so little in such a long time. It is, of
course, possible that there will be more mind later on somewhere else,
but of this we have no jot of scientific evidence.*

BERTRAND RUSSELL

IN PART TWO of this book I talk about design arguments and how
they work. They do not generate knock-down arguments for the existence of God or any kind of "superintellect monkeying with the physics." If we follow the evidence where it leads and no further, then the
evidence does not take us to God. But it does take us part way.

There are, however, two major problems with design arguments that
have to be taken seriously: (1) Alternative explanations for design exist
with no simple way to rule them out. (2) Counterarguments *against*
design exist. If we take design seriously—based on evidence—we must
go all the way and take *all* the evidence seriously. We cannot just pick
features of the world that support our belief in God and set aside those
that do not.

Christians eager to find proof for the existence of God often have
jumped too quickly on the design bandwagon and turned it into a marvelously appealing argument—provided you don't look at it too closely.
On the other hand, with caution, the wonder and design of the universe
can play a constructive role in faith, if approached with humility and an
appropriately biblical starting point. The Bible, for example, does not
start with an examination of the natural world and conclude that there
must be a God. Rather, the biblical witness begins with the reality of
God and uses that all-encompassing reality to understand the significance of the natural world. A Christian worldview thus starts from a
foundation of faith in God and works out from there, or perhaps I
should say *down* from there. It does not start from inspection of the
world and work up to God.

Maintaining this distinction is important because of the *limitations*
of science. Science, for all its robust power to figure out what the world

is like, is silent on questions of purpose and meaning. Science provides no bridge by which we pass from inspection of the world to any grand conclusion about why the world is or why we are here or how we should live. We can note, as we have so far in this book, that science has uncovered a world that looks suggestively congenial to life. But, to note a most elementary caution, the life that the universe enables, for all science can say, could be that of the cockroach and not human beings. The carbon resonance is just as critical in making the world habitable to cockroaches as it is for humans.

Science can uncover *nothing* to suggest that humans are more relevant in the grand scheme of things than cockroaches. Humans are more complex, but why is complexity relevant? Humans beings produce art, music and language, but why are they important? Humans could probably drive the cockroach to extinction with enough effort, rather than vice versa, but so what? The humble cockroach has its virtues as well. Its simplicity and flexible diet make it robust against catastrophe. We could imagine disasters that would drive the human race to extinction and leave the humble cockroach to carry on. Furthermore, human beings are capable of destroying all the life on the planet. Perhaps humans should be viewed as the collateral damage of the universe—a reckless, irresponsible species capable of undoing all the effort it took to

Figures I.10-11. The universe has to be well designed to accommodate either a cockroach or a human being. Science can offer no guidance in suggesting which is more important. (Cockroach: Colin Ybarra/Wikimedia Commons; girl: Karl Giberson)

enable the diversity of life in the first place. I don't believe this for one minute, but I can't say that science is very helpful on this question.

Of course, all of our intuitions reject any central role for cockroaches in understanding the purpose of the universe. But science does nothing to confirm those intuitions.

If we want to connect the value we place on human beings to the purpose of the universe, we must begin with that value and work backward into the science that makes it possible for use to even have that value. We cannot begin with the universe and work forward to that value. No scientific inference can carry us from the way the world *is* to an understanding of *why* it is that way.

IS THIS THE "BEST OF
ALL POSSIBLE WORLDS"?

The Design of Design Arguments

In every respect our physical theories are approximations to reality, they claim merely to be 'realistic' and so we hesitate to draw far-reaching conclusions about the ultimate nature of reality from models which must be, at some level, inaccurate descriptions of reality.

JOHN BARROW AND FRANK TIPLER

AT 9:30 A.M. ON SUNDAY, November 1, 1755—All Saints' Day—when most of Lisbon's 275,000 residents were at church, one of Portugal's worst earthquakes struck. Its three major shocks lasted for around ten minutes. The second shock was the worst, bringing down palaces, homes, shops and most of the town's more than ninety convents and forty churches. Many church roofs, including that of the town's majestic cathedral, collapsed onto worshipers. The third shock threw up a huge dust cloud, blocking the sun on what had been a gloriously clear day just minutes earlier as the city's many Christians were making their way to church.

Fires—many from candles lit by worshipers—broke out as survivors climbed out from under the wreckage and began the search for family members. The waters of the Tagus River rose up menacingly and crashed with great devastation against the densely populated waterfront. Huge crowds that had sought shelter from falling buildings scurried to the harbor, where they drowned.

An 11 a.m. aftershock wiped out much of Western Lisbon. The Sao Paulo church, where a large crowd of refugees had gathered, was totally destroyed. An aftershock at noon damaged the northern part of the city. The effects of the earthquake were felt across the southwest of Spain, and as far away as Bordeaux in France.

Somewhere between ten thousand and sixty thousand people died from the earthquake. Christians, especially the Jesuits, suggested the disaster was a punishment from God for Lisbon's sinfulness. It was never clear, though, why Lisbon deserved this punishment any more than any other city. In fact, Lisbon was widely regarded as an unusually pious city.

The earthquake in Lisbon occurred less than three decades after the death of Isaac Newton. Europe was still deeply religious, and secularization had not yet had much of an effect on people's thinking. But Europe was gradually becoming scientific and developing a worldview that included a belief in science; a part of this belief was an intuition

Figure 7.1. A 1755 German copperplate image, *The Ruins of Lisbon*, shows people being hanged, probably for looting after the quake, as well as general mayhem after the earthquake. Priests can be seen giving the last rites to people being hanged. (The city of Lisbon during the Earthquake of 1755 [engraving] [b/w photo], German School [18th century] / Private Collection / The Bridgeman Art Library International. Used by permission.)

that the world ran according to natural laws rather than the constant intervention of God. Some believed that the Lisbon earthquake was simply a natural occurrence, no different than the changing of the seasons or the falling of the rain. It was not a judgment from God.

A natural explanation for earthquakes—the shifting of tectonic plates—would eventually be discovered. Such explanations in many areas of life were replacing the wrath of God as the explanation for natural disasters like earthquakes, floods and volcanoes. The Lisbon earthquake provided a theological laboratory where two very different understandings of the world—one ancient and one modern—were weighed in the balances and compared.

LISBON AND THE PROVIDENCE OF GOD

The Lisbon earthquake showed that the question of
whether nature is beautiful and well-organized or,
alternatively, evil, cannot be answered so simply.

CLAUDIA SANIDES-KOHLRAUSCH

THE LISBON EARTHQUAKE got a lot of attention. Of particular interest was a well-known argument from the great philosopher and mathematician Gottfried Leibniz. Leibniz had argued, quite convincingly, that the world was optimally designed—"the best of all possible worlds," as he put it.

In the wake of great disasters Leibniz's argument was easy to ridicule. After all, who can stand in the midst of a natural disaster, surrounding by burning homes and dead children calmly proclaiming, "We live in the best of all possible worlds"? The implausibility of this argument, in fact, inspired one of the greatest satirical novels of all time, *Candide*, by the French intellectual Voltaire. In *Candide*, Voltaire recounts the adventures of the colorful Dr. Pangloss, a caricature of Leibniz. Pangloss was a mouthpiece parodying a popular argument of that time—namely that we live in the best of all possible worlds.

In *Candide*, Voltaire explored the age-old problem of evil, the most serious intellectual objection to Christianity. The world God created has plagues, earthquakes, tornadoes and volcanoes that produce untold human suffering for no apparent reason. So, as the argument goes, there is either no God and these events are without meaning, or he is not a good God and doesn't care about human suffering, or he is a powerless God who can't prevent even the most terrible of evil disasters. In a larger sense, however, *Candide* is about the design argument that we are exploring in this book. Leibniz argued that this world is full of discernable purpose, and if we look at things in just the right way, we can see God's purposes. Voltaire's Pangloss saw the world as a hyperbolic caricature of this argument, discerning purposes everywhere, even where there clearly were none.

Figures 7.2-3. Gottfried Wilhelm Leibniz (1646-1716), left, was one of Germany's leading intellectuals in the seventeenth century and codiscoverer of the calculus, with Newton. François-Marie Arouet (1694-1778), who wrote under the pen name Voltaire, was a leading French Enlightenment thinker and social reformer. (Leibniz: Johann Friedrich Wentzel d. Ä./Wikimedia Commons; Voltaire: Engraving by Baquoy, ca. 1795/Wikimedia Commons)

"It is demonstrable," says Dr. Pangloss, "that things cannot be otherwise than as they are; for as all things have been created for some end, they must necessarily be created for the best end. Observe, for instance, the nose is formed for spectacles, therefore we wear spectacles. The legs are visibly designed for stockings, accordingly we wear stockings."[1]

These arguments mock the idea that simply because things appear to have a sensible function—like our noses holding our glasses—they were designed to have that function.

IS THIS THE BEST OF ALL POSSIBLE WORLDS?

I have lived eighty years of life and know nothing for it,
but to be resigned and tell myself that flies are born to be eaten
by spiders and man to be devoured by sorrow.

VOLTAIRE

WHO CAN DOUBT that our universe is remarkably suited for life? We are tempted to conclude, after the survey of part one, that the universe is designed *for* life. We live—don't we?—in a finely tuned Goldilocks universe on a Goldilocks planet orbiting about a Goldilocks star. The design of our universe *seems* crystal clear. Change anything, even in an effort to make things better, and we are likely to end up in a sterile universe, inhospitable to life. The knobs of the universe are all set exactly right.

This was Leibniz's argument—all things considered, we live in the "best of all possible worlds," at least in terms of the laws of nature. We might even say we live in the "only possible world." Viewed objectively, and not in the middle of an unrepresentative devastation like the Lisbon earthquake, his argument is compelling. Take water, for example, which we marveled at in chapter five. Water can do many things—cool us, clean us, carry us on yachts to beautiful islands. Children can swim and play in it. But water can also drown us, as hapless Lisbonites found when the Tagus River rose up and engulfed them. So what do we make of water? Should we be grateful for water and marvel that it is a part of God's creative plan? Or should we use the fact that water drowns people as an argument against the goodness of God? Will the best of all possible worlds have water in it? Can the Lisbon mother holding her drowned child marvel at the wonder of water?

What about gravity? It holds us and the air we breathe on the surface of the earth. But it also accelerates us to our death when we fall off a cliff. It gathered raw material into the globe of the earth and produced the tectonic plates that slipped in the Lisbon earthquake. Is gravity a good thing? Again, don't ask a mother holding a child crushed by a falling building. How about electricity? It keeps the atoms and molecules in our bodies doing what they need to do to. All biological processes—all of them—involve electricity. But it also produces lightening, which occasionally destroys things and once in a blue moon kills people.

The characteristics of the world form a complicated and interlocking machine, but most of those properties—maybe even all of them—enable life in some way. If we someday begin to colonize distant planets and find one with both water and gravity like the earth, our response will be "Great! We can flourish here." We would look askance at a member of our party who said, "Gee, I was hoping for a planet without water so I wouldn't have to worry about drowning. And that gravity will be a problem if I fall off a cliff. Please tell me there is no electricity here; I hate getting shocks."

The shifting of tectonic plates caused the great Lisbon earthquake of 1755, although the residents could not have known this at the time. The surface of the earth is not a single piece of geology but rather a set of vast plates with boundaries that rub against each other along so-called fault lines. These continent-sized plates move slowly over the centuries, and occasionally stresses build up and they shift violently, producing an earthquake. The effect is much like pushing a heavy piece of furniture, which seems fixed to the floor and then suddenly slides. Earthquakes occur along these fault lines, and the modern science of earthquakes—*seismography*—does a good job of anticipating *where* and sometimes even *when* major events are likely to occur. The shifting of tectonic plates, like gravity and water, is both beneficial and dangerous. The benefit comes from the way that the motion of tectonic plates brings valuable materials, including water, up from the depths of the earth. The downside, of course, is earthquakes. But now that we know where the faults lines are, nobody has to live near them. I live in Boston, where earthquakes are so rare we don't even think about them.

Considerations such as these force a certain humility and puzzlement on us as we consider the universe and its apparent design. There

Figure 7.4-5. Hugh Ross, left, and Christopher Hitchens draw polar opposite conclusions about the universe. Ross sees a universe lovingly crafted by God to support human life. Hitchens sees a hostile cosmos with a few incidental spots where life might arise randomly. (Ross: used courtesy of Reasons to Believe; Hitchens: Andrew Rusk/Wikimedia Commons)

are those who look at the exceptional character of our wondrously habitable planet in the light of the rest of the universe, which seems rather hostile to life. Surely this entire cosmos—or even our entire solar system—cannot have its purpose fulfilled by one species on a pale blue dot orbiting a mundane star in the suburbs of the Milky Way galaxy.

Christopher Hitchens, our generation's most tireless crusader for atheism, has debated the existence of God with countless theists, from Alister McGrath to William Dembski. His perspective on our role in this vast universe, honed in the fires of his countless debates, is that "only the most extraordinarily self-centered species, could imagine that all this was going on for our sake."[2] In dramatic contrast to that caution, the popular Christian apologist Hugh Ross argues that the fine-tuning of the Goldilocks universe, with all its vast complexity, points clearly to God's providential care for humans: "Evidently God cared so much for living creatures," writes Ross, "that he constructed 100 billion trillion stars and carefully crafted them throughout the age of the universe so that at this brief moment in the history of the cosmos humans could exist and have a pleasant place to live."[3] A starker contrast would be hard to find.

HOW DO DESIGN ARGUMENTS WORK?

For all ages proofs of the wisdom and power of Him who governs the
universe have been formed by those who applied themselves to the study of it.
The greater the progress in physics, the more numerous have these proofs become.

MAUPERTUIS

DESIGN ARGUMENTS HAVE been around forever and expressed in various ways. Most of them fall into what we call *natural theology*, which is the process of inferring something about the existence and character of God by the inspection of nature. The story of creation in Genesis launches the discussion in the Judeo-Christian tradition when it speaks of God ordering nature and driving back chaos. On the fourth day God created the sun, moon, and the stars to give light to the earth and "to separate the day from the night, and let them serve as signs to mark sacred times, and days and years" (Gen 1:14 NIV). All this suggests design and purpose. Job speaks of God making "waterdrops evaporate" so the clouds can "shower abundantly on mankind." (Job 36:27-28 HCSB). The psalmist expresses awe at the grandeur of the night sky but remarkably does not comment on the grandeur of his own existence:

When I observe Your heavens,
  the work of Your fingers, . . .
what is man that You remember him? (Ps 8:3-4 HCSB)

In the New Testament, Paul speaks of the created order testifying clearly to the reality of God, arguing that "the invisible things of [God] from the creation of the world are clearly seen, being understood by the things that are made" (Rom 1:20 KJV). Biblical scholars have interpreted this to mean that an open-minded seeker can infer the existence of God by studying the creation.

As theologians reflected on the nature of the creation these arguments were repeated and refined. Augustine in the fourth century, Thomas Aquinas in the thirteenth century, Luther and Calvin at the time of the Reformation in the sixteenth century—all were understandably convinced that the world had a grand design that was readily discernible. After all, nobody had any other explanation for why birds were adapted to fly, fish to swim and constellations to mark the seasons.

By the time we get to Isaac Newton in the latter part of the seventeenth century, we have the first carefully constructed scientific arguments. Newton, as we saw earlier—and learned in high school—explained how gravity from the sun keeps the planets in their orbits. This explanation replaced previous medieval explanations that included the possibility that the planets moved because angels pushed on them. (It also replaced Galileo's explanation that they moved because of a "circular inertia," which turned out to be as much a fantasy as the pushing angels.) But Newton's theory didn't explain why the planets all go around the sun in the same direction and in almost the same plane. In fact Newton could not imagine *any* natural process that could produce such elegant design, so he argued that God must be the explanation.

Figure 7.6. William Paley, whose work on natural theology was so well known to Darwin that he could quote many passages from his book. "The marks of design are too strong to be got over. Design must have had a designer," wrote Paley. "That designer must have been a person. That person is GOD." (Paul D. Stewart/Science Photo Library. Used by permission.)

About two centuries later the most famous design argument was developed by William Paley whose *Natural Theology* Darwin read voraciously as a young scientist. "Suppose I had found a watch upon the ground," asked Paley, "and it should be inquired how the watch happened to be in that place. . . . [W]hen we come to inspect the watch, we perceive . . . that its several parts are framed and put together for a purpose. . . . [T]he inference, we think, is inevitable, that the watch must have had a maker."[4] Paley goes on to compare the watch to an eye, arguing that if a watch implies a watchmaker, then an eye implies an eye-maker. The eye-maker, of course, can only be God.

Newton's argument about the planets and Paley's about the watch have the same logical form: We find something in nature that appears too ingeniously constructed to have been produced by known natural processes, so we infer that a Designer from outside the natural order—God—must be the source of the design. Their arguments differ, however, on the question of *purpose*. It was not clear to Newton or anyone of his day exactly *why* the planets needed to be going about in the orderly way they were observed. If the order was indeed provided by God, no explanation for it could be discerned other than the creation of order for the sake of order. In contrast, the designs that Paley highlighted were clearly purposeful. Our eye is remarkably designed for a purpose other than to elicit awe at its complexity. We *see* with our eyes. We don't do anything with Neptune's nice orbit, other than admire it.

DESIGNER ARGUMENTS AND RED FLAGS

Though aware that there is nothing in the universe that suggests
any purpose for humanity, one way that we can find a purpose is to study the
universe by the methods of science, without consoling ourselves with
fairy tales about its future, or about our own.

Steven Weinberg

Arguments that the universe is designed, as I have hopefully made clear from this chapter, are complicated. We certainly live in a remarkable universe with many features that inspire awe. Many of those features connect in astonishing ways to the habitability of the universe. The psalmist's wonder at the heavens has only grown stronger as we have learned more about those heavens. The universe certainly does not become ever more boring and bland as we come to understand it.

But we also live in a world with earthquakes, plagues and tsunamis. Our sun will burn out at some point, incinerating the earth in the process. The prospects of securing our future by colonizing other planets seem remote. The long-term prognosis of the universe, by the cold logical lights of science, is not good. Its temperature will continuously drop as it expands for billions of years. Eventually there won't be enough heat left for any form of life, and finally there won't even be enough heat for atoms and molecules to interact. This sterile icy blackness is frightening to contemplate. No matter what we do as a species, we and our cultural achievements are destined to perish.

No simple overriding explanation that makes sense of *everything* comes into view as we learn more about the universe. And experience with past arguments raises red caution flags. For example, Newton's design argument about the planets was an argument from ignorance that now bears the label "god of the gaps." There was a gap in Newton's explanation for the planets. He could explain why their orbits were elliptical and what kept them in their orbits. But he could not explain the uniformity of their orbits, so he invoked God as the explanation to plug this gap—hence the label for such arguments: god of the gaps.

A century after Newton, French physicist Pierre Simon de Laplace dispelled the mystery of the structure of the solar system. He showed that a better understanding of gravity and how solar systems originate could explain the things that Newton attributed to the direct action of God. Laplace's work did not refute the existence of God, of course. But it did dismantle Newton's argument that the planetary orbits must have been set up by God, thus eliminating an argument that some had been using to defend God's existence (see insert figure P).

In a similar way, Darwin's theory of evolution offers an explanation for the design that Paley marveled at in the eye. Scholars of Paley's generation knew nothing of natural selection, mutations or genetics, so they could not imagine how nature might craft something so remarkable as an eye. Paley's argument, like Newton's, turns out to be another god-of-the-gaps explanation that disappears with further scientific insights into the way the world works.

So this is the first red flag to note—design arguments are all-too-often based on gaps in our knowledge and will disappear when those gaps are filled.

The second red flag concerns the apparent purpose of any design. "Design" can point in many directions or no direction at all. The science museum in Boston has a grand contraption that does nothing except move balls around to no end. The only possible purpose is to impress a visitor with the juxtaposition of mechanical complexity design and lack of purpose. There is likewise no significance to the patterns of the stars that we call constellations. The "design" of the Big Dipper is simply interesting. The fine-tuning of the universe for life, on the other hand, encourages us to wonder if life may be important in some way. But it does not specify which life forms are relevant and why. And we must note that some features of our world exhibiting a high level of design—like the AIDS virus or the poison of the rattlesnake—seem to have the purpose to destroy human life. If rattlesnakes could reflect on their existence, they could marvel at the carbon resonance that makes that existence possible.

A third red flag is bad design. If marvelous design in the universe motivates reflection on the possibility that God created the world what do we do about counterarguments? Consider asteroids. A gigantic asteroid struck the Yucatan Peninsula 65 million years ago and so disrupted the ecosystems and the atmosphere of the earth that the dinosaurs—and many other species—went extinct. Nothing prevents the same thing from happening again. We are protected today largely by the vastness of space and the structure of our solar system with large outer planets that "vacuum up" a lot of stuff that could hit the earth. These protections make collisions of the sort that wiped out the dinosaurs unlikely. But they offer no guarantees. If the Goldilocks features of our universe are intended to make it habitable, then why does the universe also have anti-Goldilocks features (see insert figure Q)?

Many such issues complicate the process of figuring out why the universe is the way it is. And as we have learned somewhat reluctantly in the last few centuries, the great explanatory power of science disappears entirely when questions of purpose enter the conversation. Science is quite extraordinary at telling us *how* the world is but quite unable to tell us *why* the world is like that. Science illuminates the remarkable features of our universe that make life possible, but it goes silent when we ask whether any particular life form is the reason why the universe is the way it is. That deeply religious question has to be explored somewhere else.

These challenges caution us against naively selecting—cherry-picking we call it—a few Goldilocks features of the universe, assuming the friendly design work is for our benefit, and jumping to the conclusion that everything points simply and unambiguously in the direction of God as Creator.

IN THE BEGINNING? OR NOT?

More appropriate, I should think, is the view that God created the universe out of an interest in spontaneous creativity—that he wanted nature to produce surprises, phenomena that he himself could not have foreseen. What would such a creative universe look like?

TIMOTHY FERRIS

PERHAPS THE GREATEST ambiguity in looking at design arguments is the distinction between features of the universe that are clearly built-in and those that result, at least partially, from happenstance. Built-in features of the universe create a *necessity* for the universe to unfold in certain ways. For example, a law specifying that electrical charge cannot be created or destroyed guarantees that, no matter what happens over the course of billions of years, there will be no gain or loss of electrical charge in the universe.

In contrast to *necessary* features of the universe, there are many *contingent* features. The best example would be the location of our planet in the middle of a habitable zone. It is not *necessary* that planets form in such a zone. No law exists that specifies where planets will form around a star. We know that planetary systems like ours form from the clouds of debris created when stars explode. We know this provides planets with water, carbon and other materials necessary for life. Such things necessarily follow from the laws that describe the formation and evolution of stars and solar systems. But there exists no law specifying *where* planets form as gravity collects the material around the star into huge balls. Nonetheless, life is *contingent* upon planets forming in such zones. The earth formed in the habitable zone—lucky for us. It didn't have to form there, though.

Of course, with trillions of stars, plenty of habitable zones exist throughout the universe. The formation of one earthlike planet in this vast cosmic sea of possibilities is close to a sure thing—but it is not guaranteed. And if we assume that life such as ours is somehow the "goal" of the universe, we have to note the many other contingencies along the way, from the moment the universe began to the emergence of life. A habitable planet could easily become uninhabitable if struck by an asteroid. Life forms can be destroyed by viruses or climate change. The conditions that give rise to life are often fragile and improbable. How can we be sure such conditions will be available when needed?

Life forms like ours require a synergistic combination of necessary and contingent events to occur along an unfolding path. Our universe must be born with certain laws of physics and chemistry. Without those laws, no life of any sort will be possible. But those laws merely provide a *framework* for the course of events. They empower the universe to evolve in the direction of life, but they do not guarantee that it will do so.

As I write these words, a great debate rages in Congress about tax rates, which illustrates this conundrum. Most politicians believe that lower tax rates will be good for the economy, which struggles now with high unemployment. Lower taxes mean more money for people to spend on products. Buying more products creates demand and people will have to be hired to build those products. The wild card in this scenario, however, is what people will *do* with their money. If people are to *spend* more money without having to borrow it, they need to *have* more money. That is *necessarily* true. But whether they actually spend the money, and what they spend it on, is *contingent*. If people put their extra money in a coffee can under the sink or send it to their relatives in Central America, then that money will not energize the American economy. The desired outcome is a combination of necessary and contingent events.

The cosmic story that proceeds from the big bang to the present is a mixture of very different sorts of ingredients—fundamental laws of physics, initial conditions that got things going in a certain way, highly probable contingent events and some happenstance. It is a wonderful story—an absolutely "Thank God it's true" story. But it's also a complex story, and difficult to interpret.

FOLLOWING THE EVIDENCE

Is There Purpose in the Universe?

The universe was brought into being in a less than fully-formed state,
but was gifted with the capacity to transform itself from unformed
matter into a truly marvelous array of structure and life forms.

St. Augustine

THE FINELY TUNED CHARACTER of our universe, with its many
Goldilocks features enabling life, is called the anthropic principle. The
most substantial work on the topic is John Barrow and Frank Tipler's
definitive *The Anthropic Cosmological Principle* that, in more than seven
hundred pages and fifteen hundred references, details the many features of our universe necessary for life. It is the most ambitious and
scholarly work I have ever read.

The term *anthropic principle* is an unfortunate misnomer. It comes
from the ancient Greek term *anthropos*, which means "man" or "human."
The problem with this description, as we saw earlier, is that none of the
anthropic features of the universe point to humans any more than cockroaches or rattlesnakes. A purely scientific interpretation of the data
could be that our universe has the conditions for life in a general sense
and that various random life forms have emerged as a result. Human
beings, in this view, are just byproducts of a universe that did not have
them in mind.

The seemingly random process of biological evolution further motivates such sentiments. In this chapter though, I argue that the history of life on this planet is neither random nor purposeless. In doing so, I start by accepting that the biological theory of evolution is basically true, as Francis Collins and I laid out in *The Language of Faith and Science*, published in 2011, or I argued in *Saving Darwin: How to Be a Christian and Believe in Evolution*, published in 2008. Readers uncomfortable with evolution are encouraged to read these or any of the books by Christians who have made peace with evolution. In the meantime, I suggest suspending skepticism and see, in C. S. Lewis's great phrase, "where the argument leads."

DOES EVOLUTION HAVE A DIRECTION?

We are the accidental result of an unplanned process . . .
the fragile result of an enormous concatenation of improbabilities,
not the predictable product of any definite process.

STEPHEN JAY GOULD

MANY CONSIDER THE belief that the life forms on our planet evolved without any direction to be central to the theory of evolution. Some evolutionists react with great hostility to suggestions that there might be anything built into nature creating preferred directions. And, of course, the idea that God might be involved in guiding the process is treated as a form of scientific hate speech. Biological evolution is based on changes in DNA called genetic mutations, which happen randomly as near as we can tell. Some of these changes result in slightly different organisms that reproduce more efficiently—a process called *differential reproduction*—and those mutations will thus become more common as offspring with those mutations grow in population.

Some quite natural and entirely reasonable questions arise from this definition of evolution: (1) Are all mutations equally probable? Do we know enough to rule out directionality at this level? Could God work through the laws of biochemistry to induce desired mutations? (2) Does differential reproduction create a direction? Even if mutations are entirely random, reproduction is not. Those organisms that are most fit have more offspring. Shouldn't "fitness" be steadily increasing, creating a direction? And finally there is the central theological question: (3) Can evolution be guided by God in any way?

The late Stephen Jay Gould emphasized the random, contingent character of evolution: "Alter any early event, ever so slightly and without apparent importance at the time, and evolution cascades into a radically different channel."[1] It seems, therefore, if the DNA in our

Figure 8.1. Stephen Jay Gould was highly critical of images like this that suggested that evolution not only had a "direction" but that simpler creatures were somehow "looking ahead" and trying to reach the next level. (Used with permission. ©Aleksander1/depositphotos)

history had gone in a slightly different direction, a very different species may have evolved. "Replay the tape a million times from [the] beginning," writes Gould, "and I doubt that anything like Homo sapiens would ever evolve again."[2]

Many share Gould's view. He was a gifted writer and an influential science popularizer. His view, however, was the most extreme that could be adopted and went beyond the scientific evidence. The opposing view, ironically, is that of Simon Conway Morris, whose work Gould praises in *Wonderful Life,* the very book where he argues for the happenstance character of evolution.[3] One of the world's leading paleontologists, Conway Morris, argues opposite to Gould. He believes that humans, or a humanlike species, are actually an *inevitable* part of evolution.

Conway Morris does not propose a different mechanism for evolution. He merely argues—on the basis of the same evidence that Gould used—for a different interpretation of its outcomes. He agrees with Gould that evolution could have taken various paths, but he argues that each of those paths would lead to something like the human species.

Here is Conway Morris's argument:

The prevailing view of evolution is that life has no direction—no goals, no predictable outcomes. Hedged in by circumstances and coincidence, the course of life lurches from one point to another. It is pure chance that 3 billion years of evolution on Earth have produced a peculiarly clever ape. We may find distant echoes of our aptitude for tool making and language and our relentless curiosity in other animals, but intelligence like ours is very special. Right?

Wrong! The history of life on Earth appears impossibly complex and unpredictable, but take a closer look and you'll find a deep structure. Physics and chemistry dictate that many things simply are not possible, and these constraints extend to biology. The solution to a particular biological problem can often only be handled in one of a few ways, which is why when you examine the tapestry of evolution you see the same patterns emerging over and over again.[4]

In *Life's Solution: Inevitable Humans in a Lonely Universe*, Conway Morris describes similar physical traits or abilities found among completely dif-

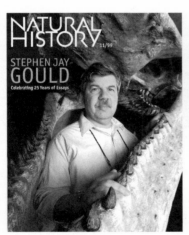

Figures 8.2-3. Stephen Jay Gould and Simon Conway Morris (right) were both leading evolutionary biologists at major universities, with great respect for each other. Despite this, they drew completely opposite conclusions about the nature of evolutionary change. Gould thought evolution was totally random; Conway Morris thought it had a direction. (Dudley Simons/University of Cambridge)

ferent species.[5] Such similarities can be easily explained if the species have common ancestors. Human and chimpanzee genomes are almost identical, which explains why those species are so similar. But this is not mysterious in any way, since humans and chimpanzees had a common ancestor from which they inherited their many shared features. But Conway Morris chooses examples that are so distantly related that common ancestry is not a feasible explanation for shared characteristics. He argues that complex traits have independently evolved in several different species.

The eye is an example. Other species have visual systems similar to ours, including, if you can imagine it, the octopus.[6] Humans and octopuses have unrelated ancestors, however, neither of which had an eye like the one they share. The most *reasonable* interpretation of the evidence suggests that two independent evolutionary paths led to the same eye structure. If this is true, then we have to ask: How can unrelated and random processes lead to the same complex final destination?

If evolution is completely contingent, such convergences are all the more improbable. Conway

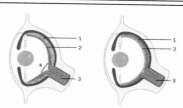

Figure 8.4. The vertebrate eye, left, evolved separately from the octopus eye, right, and yet the similarities are extraordinary, suggesting that there must be some preferred pathway for natural selection that leads to a common result. Ironically, the octopus eye lacks the defect of the blind spot that we have in our eyes. On the left the nerve fibers (2) pass in front of the retina, and there is a blind spot (4) where the nerves pass through the retina. In vertebrates, 1 represents the retina and 2 is the nerve fibers, including the optic nerve (3), whereas in the octopus eye, 1 and 2 represent the nerve fibers and retina respectively. The octopus arrangement avoids a blind spot. (Caerbannog/Wikimedia Commons)

Morris argues that the laws of nature allow for only a few solutions to any particular problem. Nature is structured so it favors these outcomes. The eye—with all its remarkable complexity—has developed independently at least seven times. This is a provocative insight. Conway Morris, and those who share his views, argue that there are certain *favored* pathways in the history of life that suggests that evolution can have preferred directions. These favored pathways exist independently of evolution. In fact, they precede the appearance of life.

COULD CONVERGENCE LEAD TO HUMANS?

Man is . . . related inextricably to all reality, known and unknowable . . .
plankton, a shimmering phosphorescence on the sea and the spinning planets
and an expanding universe, all bound together by the elastic string of time.

JOHN STEINBECK

IF CONVERGENCE IS true, it confirms the central assumption that guides the Search for Extraterrestrial Intelligence (SETI). This search, which is taken seriously by the scientific community, is conducted by listening for intelligent radio signals from space and sending signals out hoping for a response. The search assumes—significantly—that alien life forms would be much like us. They would, for example, have advanced to the point where they would be using radio technology. The existence of extraterrestrials with radio technology suggests several rather specific things: (1) They would have developed big brains, capable of understanding advanced physics and mathematics. Chimps and bonobos, as clever as they may be at piling up boxes to reach bananas or getting doors open that have M&Ms behind them, will never discover the laws of physics no matter how much time you give them. (2) They would have manual dexterity sufficient to construct high-tech equipment. Dolphins, which amaze their trainers with their many clever behaviors, could never manage a soldering iron with their flippers. (3) They would be sufficiently curious to be attracted to science and the possibility of other life forms in the universe. (4) They would have the visual sophistication to develop an idea of the universe and the possibility of life "out there." These assumptions, which undergird the SETI program and the long-running Star Trek series, suggest that life must converge in a powerful way on intelligence like ours.

Convergence is incredibly complex, of course, and much harder to understand than the carbon resonance or the other Goldilocks features of the universe. Many biologists reject it. The development of an eye is not an "event" like the fusion of helium atoms into carbon; it is a long, complex process involving thousands of meandering steps. If it were not for the fact that eyes have evolved several times, we would not be inclined to think that natural pathways would lead in that direction, given the higgledy-piggledy trajectory of the path.

Convergence is based on abstract and indirect reasoning. From the fact that nature has accomplished certain unusual feats—like making almost identical eyes more than once—we infer that there must exist something not yet understood in nature to account for that successful result. Evolutionary convergence is thus similar to Fred Hoyle's carbon resonance before it was discovered. In essence Hoyle said, "Nature seems unusually adept at making carbon. There must be something going on to explain this." By analogy, Conway Morris is saying, "Nature seems unusually adept at making eyes. There must be something going on to explain this." Convergence, however, is more complicated than carbon fusion, which was explained with a few interlocking facts about nuclear physics. Convergence—if there is such a thing—is an indirect statistical process that might, in the short run, be completely invisible but over millions of years be seen to move in certain predictable directions. This, however, makes evolutionary convergence eerily similar to cosmic fine-tuning. The fine-tuning of the universe is not visible from moment to moment. An observer of the hydrogen-dominated early universe would not be expected to predict that "Someday there will be more than a hundred elements." Looking back, we can see that this possibility was built into the laws, but because the processes unfolded in such a slow and irregular way, we could never have anticipated it. In the same way, we could not imagine an observer of the first life on earth to predict that "Some day there will be hundreds of creatures with eyes and brains, running, flying and swimming about." But that is what we see with those remarkable eyes we have.

Conway Morris suggests that convergent human characteristics include our abilities to balance ourselves, detect sounds and process visual information. And highly developed brains are probably convergent. Conway Morris is a respected evolutionary biologist with a prestigious appointment at Cambridge University. He is not a fringe biologist with dubious credentials. And yet, following the evidence where it leads, he is convinced that creatures with large brains capable of consciousness, language and complex thought would *inevitably* emerge from the evolutionary process: "Contrary to popular belief, the science of evolution does not belittle us," he writes. "Something like ourselves is an evolutionary inevitability, and our existence also reaffirms our one-ness with the rest of Creation."[7]

This is a critical insight into the possibility that God created life through gradual processes deeply embedded in the natural order. In reflecting on the significance of this, Francis Collins and I argue:

> The exact anatomical features of sentient creatures like ourselves might not be precisely specified by the evolutionary process, of course. The playing field of natural history, as Morris argues, is tilted in the direction of big brains and remarkable eyes, but there is no evidence that evolution prefers hands with five fingers, ears five feet above the ground, or noses below the eyes rather than above.
>
> Many find this thought unsettling and strangely at odds with their understanding of creation, which celebrates that God created us "in his image." We suggest that this is due to the influence that actual artistic images have had on our view of God and ourselves. Because God became incarnate in Jesus, who looks like us, we all too quickly slip into the assumption that God also looks like us. After all, fathers generally resemble their sons! Religious art, like the anthropomorphic paintings of God on the Sistine Chapel, feed into this assumption that God looks like us. But we know, upon reflection, that these intuitions cannot be correct. God does not have hands and feet. He is not a bipedal mammal with a big brain. Whatever meaning we attach to our belief that we are in the image of God, we most certainly cannot claim that our physical bodies somehow resemble God's body.[8]

EVOLUTION AS A NONZERO-SUM GAME

Might not the evolutionary process, despite its contingency, still be consonant with the achievement of purpose on the part of a creator God?

ALISTER MCGRATH

ONE OF THE most provocative and theologically suggestive books published in the last several years is Robert Wright's *Nonzero: The Logic of Human Destiny.* In *Nonzero,* Wright argues, on the basis of a branch of mathematics known as *game theory,* that reality operates on a tilted playing field that favors certain outcomes. Wright, who was raised Southern Baptist but is no longer a Christian, speculates that God created the world in such a way that social and biological events will unfold in a certain direction. *Nonzero* unfolds his vision of an optimistic trajectory for both the biological evolution of our species and our political and economic history.

Wright says that "nonzero-sumness" "gives a certain momentum to the basic direction of life on this planet. It explains why biological evolution, given enough time, was likely to create highly intelligent life—life smart enough to generate technology and other forms of culture. It also explains why the ensuing evolution of technology, and of culture more broadly, was very likely to enrich and expand the social structure of that intelligent species, carrying social organization to planetary breadth," and creating the global village of today.[9]

The game theory invoked by Wright studies behavior patterns and

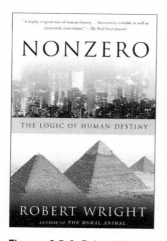

Figures 8.5-6. Robert Wright's book *Nonzero* was a *New York Times Book Review* Notable Book in the year 2000 and has been published in nine languages. *Fortune* magazine included *Nonzero* on a list of "the 75 smartest [business-related] books of all time." (Photo courtesy of Robert Wright)

informal rules of the sort that we use every day in our interactions with each other. Why do we hold doors open for people? Why do we let someone put their coat on a preferred seat and "own" that seat while they go do other things? Why does the first person to yell "shotgun" get to sit in the front of the car? Why does an entire class of students prefer to stay after school rather than tattle on the class clown who drew the picture of the teacher in a monkey costume? Every day we perform countless small actions without thinking—actions that come "naturally," whatever that means, based on habits we have picked up along the way. How do we understand this? The answer is game theory, which suggests that certain behaviors will come naturally if they lead to the best *overall* outcomes. Such outcomes are described as *nonzero-sum*, which contrasts—no surprise!—with *zero-sum*.

To see how this works we have to understand the difference between these two different kinds of outcomes. A zero-sum interaction between two people involves benefits that are fixed in such a way that one person's gain is exactly matched by another person's loss. If two children quarrel about which one should get a cookie, they do so knowing that there is just one cookie and no matter how the cookie is divided, whatever one gets is exactly equal to what the other does not get. If the only way to acquire something is to take it from someone else, or otherwise prevent him or her from getting it, then the interaction is zero-sum. Zero-sum interactions are easy to understand.

Many nonzero interactions are equally easy to understand. Suppose, for example, that the two children quarreling about the cookie decide to make a trade rather than divide the cookie. The younger child agrees to give up her share of the cookie in exchange for some help from the older child—who has cooking privileges—in making cookies. At the end of that negotiation there are more cookies to go around. Many transactions are based on the philosophy of nonzero-sumness, where both parties can come out ahead, sometimes dramatically. If my neighbor has a big riding lawnmower and a dull ax, and I have a small manual mower and a new chain saw, we can agree that he will mow my lawn and I will cut down his tree. The result is that both of our chores get done faster and we have time left over—a win-win or nonzero-sum interaction.

Game theory explains the success of free markets, which, when they work, make the whole more than the sum of the parts. In essence the free markets let everyone trade goods and service they produce effectively for goods and services that they cannot produce effectively. I educate the children of plumbers, stockbrokers and farmers in exchange for plumbing, investment advice and food. We all come out ahead.

An important byproduct of nonzero-sum interactions is the steady and growing relevance of honesty, trust and cooperation. When we enter into agreements, we have to trust each other. When we behave without integrity, we lose the trust of others and compromise our ability to enter into subsequent agreements. We are socially, economically and politically damaged by such behavior. I must be a responsible college professor or the plumber will not enroll his children at my college. If no children enroll at my college, I will have no job. If I have no job, I cannot afford to hire the plumber to put a new bathroom in my house.

Widespread cooperation between parties with a high degree of trust in their various interactions creates benefits for almost everyone. This explains why standards of living and quality of life have risen so dramatically in the past few centuries in those parts of the world where people have entered into steadily more intricate social, economic and political arrangements. Everyone benefits when one person gets paid to make all the bread for the village in his big oven rather than everyone having to make their own bread in tiny ovens. A village with a baker, a builder and a brewer will be more prosperous than a village where everyone has to bake, build and brew on their own. And everyone will enjoy better bread.

The path from a simpler past where people were more self-sufficient to the complex world of today was not a simple trajectory with steadily increasing quality of life and no stumbles. There were missteps, reversals and even wars along the way. But there can be no doubt that this path has led to an improved quality of life.

The branch of mathematics called game theory puts a quantitative face on this phenomenon. Game theory allows us to *predict* that societies will grow steadily more complex and interactive over time. And this is exactly what has happened. People have banded together with neighbors to create villages, enabling things like education, sports and sanitation. Villages and city-states have joined to create countries, enabling things like common currencies, postal systems and mutual defense. And countries are joining together into larger entities to enhance trade, ensure peace and provide mutual support in times of crisis. At the present, international cooperation facilitates global trade, fighting terrorism and working on climate issues, with varying degrees of success. The cell phones we use every day testify to the global cooperation of the modern world. The minerals come from Africa, the design from America, the construction from Asia. Our global village is built on nonzerosum interactions between countless parties who all benefit from such cooperation. All this makes perfect sense when viewed from the perspective of game theory.

Wright's nonzero argument also extends to the history of life on this planet. The argument here is of the same form but harder to see because we are not a part of the process. The argument goes like this: Life, as we understand it, began on planet earth some 3.7 billion years ago as a single cell. All the life forms on the planet were single cell. But at some point, after millions of years, single-celled life became multicellular. Although such life forms don't generally leave fossils, we can be reasonably sure that the first multicellular life was basically just a big clump of cells, all of which were quite similar.

A clump of cells, though, is not like a single cell. Some of the cells in the clump are *inside* and some are *outside*. This opens the door to specialization, where outside cells can be optimized for functions like protecting the organism from harmful germs. Our skin, for example, does a great job with this. Interior cells, by contrast, are freed from the need to interact with the outside world and can redirect their energies to other functions, like reproduction. In the same way that a village is better off when everyone doesn't have to bake their own bread and build their own furniture, an organism is better off when every cell does not have to worry about both reproduction and fending off threats.

Game theory, despite sounding like a set of ideas that might be applied to sports like tennis or board games like Monopoly, is a mathematical explanation for the behavior of complicated systems with lots of interacting parts. Game theory—and here is the provocative theological point—would exist even if there were no universes with entities embodying its insights. In this sense it is part of the deep structure of the universe—not unlike gravity or electromagnetism, or countless other branches of mathematics. Game theory suggests that individual organisms will more easily accomplish their goals by being complex and multidimensional; people will flourish in tribes rather than in isolation; tribes that cooperate will be better off than those that do not; and the playing field of the entire planet is tilted in favor of global cooperation.

Wright suggests that this viewpoint—which he defends on entirely secular grounds—supports the idea that the world might be viewed as the creation of a god who intended it to be filled with love. In his follow-up to *Nonzero*, titled *The Evolution of God*, Wright

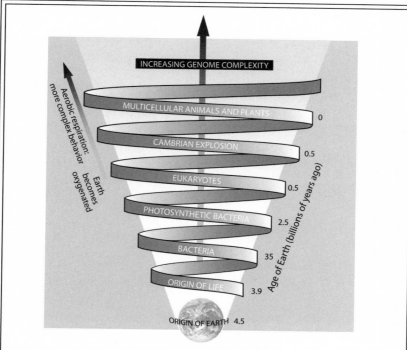

Figure 8.7. The complexity of the most complex genomes has increased steadily over time, although many simpler genomes have persisted into the present. Are there factors in nature that favor the steady increase in complexity? Or is this simply an implication of the fact that life begins in a simple form and has nowhere to go but in the direction of greater complexity?

comments on the way that nature developed creatures that learned to love each other:

> It's pretty remarkable: natural selection's invention of love—in some anonymous animal many millions of years ago—was a prerequisite for the moral imagination whose expansion, here and now, could help keep the world on track; a prerequisite for our apprehension of the truth that the planet's salvation depends on: the objective truth of seeing things from the point of view of someone else, and the moral truth of considering someone else's welfare important.[10]

Wright's speculations lend support for the belief that God created the world, although his concept of God won't warm every Christian's heart. At the heart of Christianity—and virtually all other religions—is the belief that human beings are not solitary creatures: we are created to live in communities and flourish when we are embedded in a network of loving, caring and trusting relationships. That the universe seems structured to bring this about is quite suggestive. "There is a moral axis to the universe," Wright told Salon.com in a 2009 interview. "It raises legitimate questions as to whether the whole system was in fact set up by some being, something you could call a divinity."[11]

The patterns of history suggest to Wright that "some larger purpose is unfolding through the history of life on this planet." And as for the source of that purpose? "You can use the term 'divine,' if you want," he says.[12]

FITTING THE PIECES TOGETHER

Religious belief consists of the belief that there is an unseen order and that our supreme good lies in harmoniously adjusting to that order.

William James

Simon Conway Morris, Robert Wright and the fine-tuning enthusiasts we met in previous chapters, make intriguing arguments. They suggest that the patterns of the history of life and societies on the earth reveal evidence of unfolding purpose. Before the earth was formed, before there was any life on earth, before there were any intelligent creatures, the foundations were in place for there to be intelligent, morally reflective creatures who understood the importance of loving each other.

These conclusions are best understood as *theological reflections* on the *scientific picture of the world*, although they can certainly be explored from a purely scientific perspective. The issue, as I mentioned earlier, is that the scientific perspective does not—indeed, *cannot*—tell us whether it is a good or bad thing that the laws of biochemistry are set up in such a way that eyes readily evolve or towns have bakeries or that creatures learn to love each other. Just as the carbon resonance does not explain what it is *for*, so convergence and nonzero-sumness do not explain what they are for. All we can do is look and see what sorts of things are made *possible* by these features of the universe. Having done so, however, we are certainly licensed to step back, look at the big picture and construct a comprehensive worldview that combines the scientific picture of the world with the religious affirmation that the world exists for a purpose and is not, as Shakespeare's Macbeth says, "a tale told by an idiot, full of sound and fury, but signifying nothing." I will explore what this looks like later, in chapter ten.

CAUTIOUS OPTIMISM

The Real Scoop on the
Fine-Tuning of the Universe

The simplest and most popular cosmological model today predicts that you have a twin in a galaxy about 10 to the 10^{28} meters from here.

MAX TEGMARK

IMAGINE STANDING IN FRONT of a firing squad with ten marksmen pointing rifles at you. Your hands are tied to a post and you are blindfolded. You hear the command "Fire." Your knees go weak and you collapse, passing out from fright, held up only by being tied to the post.

A few hours later you wake up in your cell, dazed and confused. The last thing you recall was hearing "Fire," followed by guns going off. You should be dead. But here you are, very much alive.

Naturally you wonder what happened. You do the standard pat-down of your body to see if it is full of holes, like they do in the movies. Your cell mate informs you that "They all missed." He goes on to explain that the warden was so puzzled by this that he had you taken back to your cell rather than set up a second execution. *How can this be?* you wonder, speculating about the odds of ten marksmen all missing a large target at almost point-blank range.

Over the next few days you ponder what happened. Various explanations come to mind; your friends suggest other possibilities that didn't occur to you. One hard-nosed skeptic with limited imagination says simply, "Of course they all missed. If they hadn't missed you wouldn't be here asking these questions." This seems clearly true, of course, but it doesn't put even a tiny dent in your curiosity. In fact there is a circularity to it that makes you wonder if your skeptical friend is saying anything more interesting than "The past must be compatible with the present."

After much reflection, your intuition remains that the proper explanation for your good fortune lies in some kind of *conspiracy*. Some benefactor must have paid off the marksmen, bribing them to miss, or maybe

Figure 9.1. No matter how improbable the result, if you have enough attempts, every possible result will happen. If you roll one hundred dice at a time, you will get at least one six virtually every time. (Used with permission. © Laurent Renault/depositphotos)

the guns were modified without the marksmen knowing, so they wouldn't shoot straight. Or maybe the marksmen were making some point to their employer, perhaps wanting a raise.

Another explanation is proposed by your mathematical friend with an unlimited imagination but few skills at navigating the real world. "What if," he asks, "there were 50,000 executions planned that day—all exactly like yours?" If there were a large number of executions, he explains, then the probability that one of them got messed up becomes much more likely. The executions then become like lottery tickets—someone will win the lottery even though the odds are stacked against them by 50,000 to one. There is no mystery to this, he says. "But were there 50,000 executions that day?" you ask. "I don't recall hearing a lot of gunfire. How can there have been 50,000 executions with no sound of gunfire?"

"There must have been," your numerical friend replies, clearly wedded to his ingenious explanation. "Otherwise how do we explain the fact that you are here?

SO WHY THE GOLDILOCKS UNIVERSE?

A potent explanation of nature's constants requires a
vast assortment of universes endowed with many
different values with those constants.

BRIAN GREENE

CANADIAN PHILOSOPHER JOHN Leslie created the provocative analogy of the firing squad to illuminate the deep puzzlement that should be evoked by the Goldilocks universe. We live in a universe with physical characteristics finely tuned for life. These characteristics have to be exactly as they are or we could not be here. Each one of them is like a marksman who has to miss at point-blank range—as unlikely as that may be—to account for your existence.

People respond very differently to the suggestion that God designed the universe for humans. The atheist Christopher Hitchens makes the counterargument, namely, that many features of this universe don't looked designed at all, and we can't simply cherry-pick those features that make our point and ignore the rest.

Richard Dawkins, a leading atheist and one of the most prominent public intellectuals of our generation, acknowledges that the universe appears designed—"as if the universe were set up to favour our eventual evolution." Like the thinkers we looked at in chapter six, he also compares the "set-up" of the universe to a machine with several knobs that "could in principle be tuned to any of a wide range of values." Dawkins objects to the suggestion that "a divine knob-twiddler must have been at work." "That explanation," he says, "is vacuous because it begs the biggest question of all. The divine knob-twiddler would himself have to have been at least as improbable as the settings of his knobs."[1]

Dawkins makes an important point that eager apologists pass over too quickly. How do we assess the probability of *God's* existence? Is the existence of God more or less probable than the existence of a finely tuned Goldilocks universe? If we cannot answer that question, then scientifically speaking we can't invoke God as the *explanation* for the

fine-tuning of the universe. Explanations in the natural sciences are
always better when *complex* effects are explained on the basis of *simpler*
causes, not the other way around. Physicists explain the origin of much
of the periodic table of elements as the result of one process—fusion. If
the explanation were in terms of an unimaginably complex "periodic
table generator," then we would immediately need to explain that process. The trajectory of scientific explanation is always to explain "more
and more" with "less and less." Kepler had three laws of planetary motion, which Newton reduced to one simple formula. The wobbly orbit
of Saturn was explained with another planet, not a new planetary wobble maker. Hoyle explained the efficient production of carbon with an
energy level of the sort that was commonly known to exist, not an entirely new theory of carbon making. This is the way of science, and it
has been very successful.

Whether this form of scientific explanation can proceed indefinitely
is an open question. I don't see how it can. It seems to me that explanation, like most things, must have boundaries where it finds itself up
against something different—something that is not an explanation.
Fine-tuning is a perfect example. We can explain so much with gravity—elliptical orbits, wobbly planets, rocket trajectories and more. We
can explain the large-scale motion of almost everything in the universe
with gravity, but we cannot explain gravity itself. Similarly, we can explain almost everything that electrons do inside atoms and molecules
with quantum mechanics, but we can't explain why the electron has the
charge that it does. Our theories seem destined to be forever partial and
incomplete, with important features that have to be added from outside
the theory. In the case of gravity, we have to actually measure the
strength of the force and then put that number into the theory if we
want it to be useful. We cannot get that number from *inside* the theory.
This contrasts with elliptical orbits, to take just one example, which can
be generated from within the theory. Even if we could not make any
observations of orbits, we would still know they had to be elliptical, on
the basis of the theory.

Physicists hold out hope that this frustrating incompleteness might
some day be resolved. In his classic, if incomprehensible, *A Brief History*

of Time, Stephen Hawking articulated this dream: "One would hope to find a complete, consistent, unified theory," he wrote almost wistfully, "that did not need to be adjusted to fit the facts by picking the values of certain arbitrary numbers in the theory."[2]

The fine-tuning of the universe is a perfect example of the limitations of scientific explanation. To make matters worse the mystery relates to the habitability of the universe, not some technical question like why Pluto has such an unusual orbit. And, going one step further, the mystery invites us to bring God into the discussion, as the explanation for the fine-tuning.

The most common pushback on the claim that God designed the cosmos is the *multiverse argument*—essentially what our ingenious mathematical friend was proposing about why we are still alive after facing a firing squad. If there is an infinity of other universes—or even a very large number—that embody every combination of the laws of nature, then we should not be surprised that we live in the one with features hospitable to life. After all, we are never surprised that we are

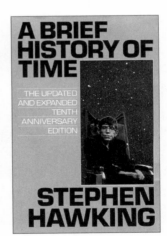

Figures 9.2-3. Stephen Hawking's runaway bestseller, *A Brief History of Time*, written in 1988, spoke optimistically—too optimistically in retrospect—of finding a theory of everything that would answer all the deep questions of the universe. He provocatively compared such a discovery with knowing the mind of God. (NASA/ Wikimedia Commons)

not living under the sea, because we would drown there. There are many locations on the earth—inside volcanoes, miles beneath the ground, the top of the highest mountain—but we are not puzzled by why we are located in a part of the earth where we can flourish, rather than die. The so-called *multi*verse—in contrast to the *uni*verse—explains our universe, just as the multiple executions explain how you didn't die in your execution event.

The multiverse is a speculative idea that emerges from mathematical physics. Many book-length treatments have looked at it, raising profound questions about the nature of both physical reality and the scientific method that investigates that reality. The basic argument is that the process that gave birth to our universe is not unusual and probably has given birth to countless other universes throughout time and space. In his 2011 book *The Hidden Reality: Parallel Universes and the Deep Laws of the Cosmos*, Columbia University physicist Brian Greene surveys no less than nine independent theoretical possibilities for multiverses. He labels them quilted, inflationary, brane, cyclic, landscape, quantum, holographic, simulated and ultimate.[3] They arise—sometimes quite naturally—from mathematical theories with levels of comprehensibility ranging from challenging to impossible.

The alternate universes are not hypothesized because we detect them directly, or even indirectly, which raises interesting questions about the role and significance of evidence. These universes are not like the planets in our solar system that exert small but detectable gravitational influences on each other. They are not even like the so-called dark matter that we infer from its gravitational influence, although we can't see it. The universes that make up the multiverse—and this includes the one we know and love—arise as *solutions* to equations, like the way that elliptical orbits of various shapes arise as solutions to Newton's equation for gravity.

One of the more promising of Greene's nine universe makers is *inflation*, inspired by evidence that our universe was born this way. The dreadfully complex physics transcends the modest ambitions of this book, but basically the idea looks like this: Einstein's theory of relativity shows how space and time are united as space-time. Quantum theory states that space-time must be a collection of tiny bubbles that physicists call space-time foam. Our universe was born when one of these foamy bubbles erupted in an unpredictable quantum event. And since there is an infinity of other bubbles, new universes should be constantly erupting. And if each universe is filled with ever more bubbles, then other universes will be constantly erupting from other bubbles, creating universes within universes, ad infinitum, like some nightmare set of Russian matryoshka dolls that can never be completely unpacked. These other bubbles are separate space-time structures, so we cannot interact with them in any way. This means, unfortunately, that we have no direct evidence that they exist. So what reason do we have to believe or even speculate that such other universes exist?

Mathematics provides the license to speculate about other universes. In the précis to a recent book on the topic, Stephen Hawking says:

> In *The Grand Design* we explain why, according to quantum theory, the cosmos does not have just a single existence, or history, but rather that every possible history of the universe exists simultaneously. We question the conventional concept of reality, posing instead a "model-dependent" theory of reality. We discuss how the laws of our particular universe are extraordinarily finely tuned so as to allow for our existence, and show why quantum theory predicts the multiverse—the idea that ours is just one of many universes that appeared spontaneously out of nothing, each with different laws of nature.[4]

Hawking makes grand claims here. But they are based on science. Quantum mechanics has been established beyond all doubt—and in the face of great opposition from luminaries like Einstein—to be the way the world works. But there is a qualification needed here. Quantum mechanics, like everything in fundamental physics, is deeply mathematical. The statements it makes about the world are in the form of equations that typically have multiple solutions. And not every solution to an equation corresponds to the real world.

Physicists have been solving such equations forever and then examining the solutions to see which ones, if any, describe the real world. Most equations have more than one solution; some have many, even an infinite number. Consider the equation for a golf ball struck by a club.

The actual path that the ball takes as it rockets off the face of the club will be one solution to the equation. But there will be another solution to the equation that will describe a very different golf ball—one that seems to be going backward in time. Freshman physics majors learn to toss these "nonphysical" solutions aside.

Physics is the art of finding equations that describe the real world, solving these equations and then matching the solution against the real world. Connecting the mathematical descriptions to the physical reality is essential and has long been the central part of mathematical physics. When Hawking says "every possible history of the universe exists simultaneously," he is assuming that every solution to the equation describes a real physical reality. His freshman physics instructor, however, probably cautioned him against this.

"Every possible history of the universe" is a remarkable set of narratives. *Possible* in this case would loosely mean "not self-contradictory." We would have universes more or less like this one but with interesting differences—the French won in North America instead of the English (so this book you are reading is titled *Le plus étonnant de l'Univers*). Hitler was successfully assassinated. You won the lottery two weeks ago. The Earth is the fourth planet out from the sun and not the third. Reality TV was never developed. And, of course, there will be universes where the laws of nature rule out the possibility of life. And universes where gravity was so strong they collapsed immediately after they were born.

These histories may be real, somewhere. If we have learned anything from physics—especially quantum mechanics—it is that lots of crazy, counterintuitive things are true. But physicists have always anchored their more speculative theories in careful observation. Kepler spent years analyzing planetary data before he stated confidently that the orbits were elliptical. When Newton was developing his theory of gravity he waited anxiously for new observational data so he could be sure he was on the right track. Quantum mechanics had a mountain of data that simply overwhelmed skeptical physicists and left them no alternative but to accept the odd new world it revealed. Unfortunately, multiverse enthusiasts have no such caution. It appears that the impossibility of finding real evidence for alternative "histories" has become a license to make confident and grandiose claims without such evidence and, of course, without fear of contradiction.

Nobody waxes more confident about the multiverse than physicist Max Tegmark, who directs the Foundational Questions Institute at MIT. In a cover story about multiverses in the May 2003 issue of *Scientific American*, he discussed the "evidence" for these other universes that could be obtained by "scrutinizing the properties of our universe." (This, of course, would be the only evidence of any sort we have access to.) He explains that this universe is fine-tuned for life because its various knobs were "established by random processes during the birth of our universe." This, says Tegmark, "suggests the existence of other universes with other values."[5]

Hawking and Tegmark lay out the options with clarity. The big bang that birthed our universe was an inevitable consequence of the laws of physics, or perhaps "metalaws" that transcend the physical theories that work in this universe. "Because there is a law such as gravity," writes Hawking, "the Universe can and will create itself from nothing. . . . Spontaneous creation is the reason there is something rather than nothing, why the universe exists, why we exist."[6] Gravity gets the process started and then quantum mechanics takes over and makes sure all possible universes, including ours, pop into existence.

And there are eight other ways to make universes.

THROUGH A GLASS DARKLY

There is not the slightest shred of reliable evidence that there is any universe other than the one we are in. No multiverse theory has so far provided a prediction that can be tested. As far as we can tell, universes are not even as plentiful as even two blackberries.

MARTIN GARDNER

I DON'T FIND these arguments convincing. They seem to be missing some basic theology and philosophy. Let me start with Hawking's assertion that the big bang was an "inevitable consequence" of gravity.

This could be true. Many things happen as a consequence of gravity—rain falls, you have weight, the earth orbits about the sun. But gravity is not *nothing*. We cannot answer the question "Why is there something rather than nothing?" by saying "gravity." Gravity is not *nothing*. Gravity is a deeply mathematical feature of our universe that does not explain itself. Our curiosity about the way things are is not satisfied by saying "gravity." And gravity is far from the only unexplained feature of our universe.

At the moment of creation our universe possessed a deeply rational set of interlocking physical laws that specified what was possible in the long, strange trip that was just beginning. We saw this in detail in previous chapters: Charge and energy would be conserved; gravity would rule at great distances; there would be two nuclear forces, both short range; particles would naturally form into atoms and molecules according the laws of quantum mechanics and electromagnetism. This profoundly rational set of physical laws is not "nothing." Getting a universe out of these laws is manifestly not *creation ex nihilo* (creation out of nothing). These laws cry out for explanation.

Tegmark's argument also seems circular in its claim that the Goldilocks features of our universe were "established by random processes." How can we know this? If it is indeed true that *random* processes determined the detailed properties of the laws of nature, how did this work? Tegmark's *assumption* that they were random leads him to propose an infinity of other universes to explain how we find ourselves in a randomly defined universe that is hospitable for life. In fact, he goes so far as to say this constitutes *evidence* for this infinity of other universes. This is a complex argument however, and requires some scrutiny.

Think back to the story of the firing squad that opened this chapter. Your survival could be explained in one of three ways: (1) sheer luck, which is too improbable to take seriously, unless you had some way of knowing all the other options had been eliminated, (2) a conspiracy in which an unknown benefactor manipulated the execution so you would survive, or (3) a vast roster of executions, so great in number that at least one of them was likely to randomly fail, as yours did. If you know with certainty that there was no benefactor, then you are compelled to number 3. But how do you know this? By analogy, how does Tegmark know that there was no "super-intellect monkeying with the physics," to use Fred Hoyle's expression? Only by assuming there is no superintellect does option 3 become a real option.

And finally we need to be careful when we start talking about an infinity of universes. The multiverse argument works only if the infinite roster of universes are all different. We must assume that the physical features of the universe are specified in some completely random way so that every time a universe pops into existence it will probably be different than the ones that preceded it. But since we cannot test our multiverse theories, we have no way of knowing if this is true. What if, for example, there is some sort of "metauniverse creation rule" that says "gravity will always have this form and strength." Or a rule that says electrons will always have the same weight. We could still get an infinity of different universes without realizing all possibilities.

Infinity is a strange mathematical creature, often wearing a mask, and always looking to fool us. Consider the set of all even numbers. There is an infinity of even numbers in that set, but not one of them is odd. If you need an odd number you can't simply go looking in any infinite set and expect to find one. An infinite number of fractions re-

Figures 9.4-5. George Ellis (born 1939), left, and Max Tegmark (born 1967), both leading physicists, approach the multiverse from opposite perspectives. Ellis speaks for a generation of older physicists alarmed at the speculative and non-empirical approach of the current generation of multiverse enthusiasts. (Photo of George Ellis is used courtesy of the author; photo of Max Tegmark is used courtesy of Justin Knight)

side between 1 and 2, but 3 will not be found there. There may be an infinity of universes, but the roster of possibilities need not have one that looks exactly like ours.

Thus the claim that a universe like ours will always be found within any infinite set of universes is simply not true. It *sounds* right, which is why so many people say "problem solved" when the design of our universe is "explained" by making our universe just one of an infinite set. Very little—perhaps nothing—about our universe is explained by the simple claim that there are an infinite number of other universes.

MULTIVERSE VERSUS DESIGN

The very nature of the scientific enterprise is at stake in the multiverse debate: the multiverse proponents are proposing weakening the nature of scientific proof in order to claim that multiverses provide a scientific explanation. This is a dangerous tactic.

GEORGE ELLIS

WIDESPREAD AGREEMENT EXISTS that our universe is fine-tuned for life. Few are inclined to assault this conclusion as Christopher Hitchens has done. Proffered explanations for fine-tuning fall into two camps: (1) there is just one universe and something transcendent—perhaps God—has determined that this universe should have life in it. (2) There is an infinity of randomly generated universes that cover all possibilities, including one like ours. Life can exist in some of these but not all of them. Paul Davies summarizes these options: "The multiverse theory seeks to replace the appearance of design by the hand of chance."[7] The design option troubles scientists, of course, since it implies a retreat into the ancient refuge of theology, a refuge many scientists believe no longer even exists. What we cannot explain with our science, we will ascribe to God. But the alternative—the untestable, assumption-ridden, multiverse theory—notes Davies, "hovers on the borderline between science and fantasy."[8]

The apparent starkness of these choices should make us uneasy. We certainly do not want to reject the multiverse in favor of a "God is the answer" response, lest advances in cosmology build a more solid foundation under the multiverse. And even if the multiverse becomes well-established, its characteristics will ultimately be derived from some set of (most likely) unexplained metalaws that govern the production of universes. From a theological point of view, universes pose no more challenges than are already posed by galaxies. Just as galaxies—once known as "island universes"—do not explain their own existence, simply because they are part of a larger ensemble, so universes will not explain their existence simply by becoming part of a larger ensemble. I find it hard to imagine that *any* explanatory scheme will *ever* take us all the way back to an ultimate beginning that will not itself need to be explained.

On the other hand, to reject the possibility that life might be a purposeful part of the universe is to adopt an agnostic stance that excludes, a priori, the possibility that there may be more to reality than simply what can be discovered by science.

I want to emphasize that the problem of the fine-tuning of the universe should not be simply collapsed into science versus religion, with science on the side of the multiverse and religion on the side of a transcendent source of order. We must not buy into this framing of the argument. When Diane Sawyer interviewed Stephen Hawking on this conflict between science and religion, Hawking's response was that "Science will win because it works."

Things are not that simple.

10

IT'S A WONDERFUL WORLD

Dear Father in heaven, I'm not a praying man, but if you're up there
and you can hear me show me the way . . . show me the way.

GEORGE BAILEY

IN THIS BOOK I HAVE LOOKED at the world predominantly through
the single lens of a scientist sifting evidence. I now conclude with some
reflections on how the world looks through the multiple lenses available
to me as a whole person seeking the deepest understanding. The "big
questions" explored in this book don't have simple answers, and I think
it is a mistake to try to weave tight arguments. Topics like God, free
will, morality, evil, the origin and fate of the universe, the purpose of
life, the source of the order in the natural world, and so forth simply do
not open up to our investigations in any complete and airtight way.

That doesn't mean, however, that we can't know anything or that we
can't have high degrees of confidence in our conclusions on many topics. It's just that all of us, scientists included, need a dose of humility as
we draw our conclusions.

Sir Arthur Eddington, the astronomer who made the celebrated
eclipse observations, coined a helpful analogy in this regard. Imagine a
fisherman, he said, catching fish every day in a net with three-inch
openings in the weave. Every night he sorts his fish and sells them.
After several years at his job the fisherman concludes that there are no
fish in the ocean shorter than three inches. His conclusion is scientific
in the sense that it is based on lots of careful observations. But he has
failed to note the limitations of his net. Even if the ocean was filled with
half-inch fish, he would never know because his net can't catch them.

We must not insist that our imperfect-knowledge "nets" capture all truth. Our knowledge quests, like the fisherman's net, are all limited. The nets used by the physicist to understand matter do not capture the nature of life; the nets used by the biologist to understand the messy complexities of life in its manifold diversity do not capture the underlying order the physicists have discovered. None of the nets employed by science capture morality and meaning.

How do we respond to the limitations of our nets? Do we conclude that there is no such thing as life because it doesn't show up in the nets of the physicist? Obviously not. Do we conclude that there is no such thing as free will because it doesn't show up in any of the various scientific nets? Some leading scientists, like Jerry Coyne, think so:

> We don't have free will, at least not in the way everyone thinks we do. We are biologically determined creatures, with "biology" conceived broadly as "genes + environments + gene/environment interactions." Our brains—and therefore our choices—are as biologically determined as are our livers or kidneys. The appearance of choice is no more "real choice" than the "appearance" of a Western movie town, with its thin storefront facades buttressed from behind, is identical to a real town. Biological determinism is a fact.[1]

IS THE UNIVERSE A BLEAK HOUSE?

That Man is the product of causes which had no prevision of the end they were achieving; that his origin, his growth, his hopes and fears, his loves and his beliefs, are but the outcome of accidental collocations of atoms; that no fire, no heroism, no intensity of thought and feeling, can preserve an individual life beyond the grave; that all the labours of the ages, all the devotion, all the inspiration, all the noonday brightness of human genius, are destined to extinction in the vast death of the solar system, and that the whole temple of Man's achievement must inevitably be buried beneath the debris of a universe in ruins—all these things, if not quite beyond dispute, are yet so nearly certain, that no philosophy which rejects them can hope to stand. Only within the scaffolding of these truths, only on the firm foundation of unyielding despair, can the soul's habitation henceforth be safely built.

BERTRAND RUSSELL

COYNE SPEAKS FOR many scientists who reject as unreal anything that can't be caught in the scientific net. By these lights, *nothing* transcends science. No fish are too small to be caught in the scientific net. Free will, eternal life and God cannot be caught in the scientific net, so they must be fantasies conjured by naive humans to meet psychological needs.

Such restricted and Spartan views of knowledge trouble me. Human beings are finite creatures, and it seems unreasonable to insist that no realities exist beyond those caught in our scientific nets. The history of science even suggests that humility is needed. How many times did scientists pronounce confidently that the earth is fixed? Or the universe ended just beyond the planets? Or there were no other galaxies? Or that the universe had no beginning? Or that matter behaved deterministically? Science constantly surprises us by pushing out its frontiers and even rearranging what we thought was familiar.

I am more interested, however, in the possibility of realities that *transcend* science rather than simply enlarge it. If, for example, there really are moral laws in the same sense that there are laws of physics, we will not discover that with science. In the same way, physicists will never find the transcendent source of the order in their equations. It seems to me that physicists—and this is my field—have discovered that their work brings them to a *boundary* in their knowledge—as opposed to a *gap*—

Figure 10.1. Paul Dirac (1902-1984), who won the Nobel Prize in 1933, was one of the greatest mathematical physicists of the twentieth century. He had a deep intuition that the mathematics that described the physical world would be *beautiful*. He wrote: "It is more important to have beauty in one's equations than to have them fit experiment. . . . It seems that if one is working from the point of view of getting beauty in one's equations, and if one has really a sound insight, one is on a sure line of progress." (Nobel Foundation/Wikimedia Commons)

beyond which lies something quite extraordinary.

Albert Einstein, in reflecting on the power of mathematical physics to describe the world, said, "The most incomprehensible thing about the universe is that it is comprehensible." Paul Dirac spoke of the value of having "beauty" in one's equations. Yet another Nobel laureate physicist, Eugene Wigner, wrote a celebrated essay about how the great utility of mathematics in science was "unreasonable." Countless physicists have wondered about the uncanny ability of mathematics to accurately describe phenomena in nature.[2]

Unfortunately, such insights are hard for nonspecialists to appreciate, particularly those whose recollections of math may not be so rosy. To illuminate this deep insight, let me offer the following parable, making use of the more familiar experience of music, rather than mathematics.

OF MUSIC AND MATH

Go down deep enough into anything and you will find mathematics.

DEAN SCHLICTER

IMAGINE THAT A friend is taking you on a stroll down a long, seemingly endless, incredibly noisy hallway. As you enter the hallway the noise is deafening, a combination of explosions, crumpling metal, loud music from incompatible genres, babies crying, talk show hosts yelling, politicians interrupting each other and so on. As you wander down the hallway, your friend explains that his company makes filters that eliminate any kind of noise, as long as they know exactly how those noises are produced.

He demonstrates the technology for you. As you cross a line marked "10" he turns on a filter that eliminates the sound of explosions. At 9 the crumpling metal disappears. By 5 there is just loud talking, babies and politicians wailing, and discordant music. At 1 there is nothing but beautiful music and a talk radio host yelling something about his taxes being too high. At 0 the talk radio noise is gone. You have come to the end of the hallway and are standing on a balcony on the opposite side of the building looking out into a dark abyss. The beautiful music seems to be coming out of the darkness.

"Impressed?" asks your guide, to which you answer, "Of course." But you can't help wondering about the beautiful music. Where is it coming from? How is it being produced? Can the high-tech filters shut it out?

"We don't know anything about this music," says your friend. "And our filters won't work on any sounds unless we know exactly how they are produced. Our technology is based on understanding the production of the sounds, not the sound itself." He turns to leave. "But aren't you puzzled by this music?" you ask. "Surely you must have some explanation for it."

"Nope," he says. "I used to wonder about the music, but, as you can see," he gestures into the abyss, "there is nothing there. I am a scientist, not a mystic. I agree that music is indeed there, but that is as far as I am willing to go. If you want to believe in some 'invisible orchestra in the abyss,' go ahead. But you won't catch me signing on to such nonsense."

I use this example because we can all identify with music, and few of us would be satisfied with the parsimonious worldview of our friend with the ingenious filters. Our impulse would be to go further, to find some way to understand, even if the evidence seemed inadequate. Few of us would think it foolish to believe in something that transcended our friend's understanding.

Now, replace "noise and sounds" in this parable with "nature," and replace the beautiful music coming from the abyss with mathematics. Nature on the surface is, to be sure, noisy and full of countless interesting things, from planets and people to protons and peas. And we can note the varied flora and fauna of our existence and explain some of it to our satisfaction. But as we apply our scientific knowledge to the world and drill down to the bedrock of our understanding, eliminating the noise and complexity of nature, we find something quite wondrous, which has been the theme of this book.

At the end of the great hallway that takes us from the social sciences to the natural sciences, through biology and chemistry and ultimately to physics—the "deepest" science—we find ourselves at last in the presence of a most beautiful and unexplained symphony of mathematics. A grandeur comes gradually into view as we get closer and closer to the foundations of our world. Across the dark abyss, this mathematics seemingly crystallizes out of nothing, explaining the world around us while remaining unexplained itself.

Contemplating the mystery of mathematics has led many great thinkers into mystical reflections that go far beyond science.

The quest for the deepest understanding of the world does not compel all of us to ponder the origin of mathematics. Many of us don't like math, have no idea what it means to say "equations rule the world," and are thus not awed by math. And the quest does not lead all of us who are awed by such mysteries into religion. But those that understand the eternal mystery of mathematics best impulsively lean over the railing into the abyss, because they know in their bones that there is something out there. Whether they encounter something depends on factors that elude many of their less imaginative peers. This ·is a deeply religious impulse: one that goes beyond science, but not one without motivation.

THE JOURNEY TOWARD THE LIGHT

Does this path have a heart?
If it does, the path is good;
if it doesn't, it is of no use.

CARLOS CASTANEDA

I HAVE TRIED in this book to be *cautious* but not *timid* in drawing connections between the wonder of the world and belief in God. I don't think the profound character of mathematics proves that God exists. But I do think it makes belief in a reality that transcends the physical world entirely reasonable and, I would argue, *necessary*. I don't see how we can deny the existence of a transcendent realm where, at the very least, the truths of mathematics eternally reside. The challenge is defending or even describing the thought process by which one moves cautiously from the mystery of mathematics to the reality of the transcendent, to the existence of God, and finally to a worldview that includes belief in the God of the Christian tradition.

Such a journey involves far more than reflection on math, of course, but there really isn't any simple road in place to even make such a journey. This does not suggest, however, that such a journey is inappropriate or can be made only by constantly taking irrational leaps of blind faith. Many thoughtful people—and I am one of them—have made that journey.

The world as we are coming to understand it is far too complex to be understood by simply collecting facts, drawing conclusions and weaving the conclusions into an all-encompassing tapestry of explanation. Careful thought demands, of course, that we pay attention to the reasoning process and watch out for errors. But as we work our way from simple experiences to deep conclusions about the way the world is, we constantly find ourselves forced to go *beyond* mere generalizations from facts. It is as though we have carefully assembled our house by following the blueprint to the letter, only to discover, as we pass through the front door, that our new house is much grander than we anticipated.

One of the twentieth-century's deepest thinkers, the Hungarian chemist-turned-philosopher Michael Polanyi, articulated this feature of our experience in his immortal phrase "we can know more than we can tell." Polanyi, who had a profound understanding of science and its limitations, argued that our quest for truth makes meaningful use of hunches, intuitions and creative imaginings. The layers of understanding that we wrap around our experiences are, by definition, larger than those experiences.

When Paul Dirac suggested that it was important to have *"beauty"* in one's equations, what did he mean? We don't even have a clear concept of mathematical beauty, much less an aesthetic yardstick to measure it. I quoted Freeman Dyson earlier as saying, "The more I examine the universe and the details of its architecture, the more evidence I find that the universe in some sense must have known we were coming."[3] What could Dyson possibly mean by this deeply metaphorical statement? What details suggested this to him?

If Dyson and Dirac were run-of-the-mill physicists working at some minor state university or apologetics project somewhere, their comments would be dismissed. But they are two of the greatest mathematical physicists in the history of science, with deep, deep insights into the world. They are rightly respected for the equations and theories they discovered and developed. But these equations and theories are just the part of what they know that can be explained. The reality is that they *know more than they can tell.*

Geniuses like Dyson and Dirac transcend their disciplines in ways that allow them to speak freely in ways denied to lesser thinkers. Their reputations are such that they can acknowledge the mysteries of the world without raising suspicions that they have some hidden quirky agenda, or that their achievements were some sort of fluke.

I have dwelt at some length on Dyson-Dirac arguments that come from mathematical physicists because this, for me, works as a helpful starting point. I am, after all, a physics geek. An artist or a social worker might find another starting point more attractive.

WINDOWS ON THE WORLD

Science and religion are two windows that people look through,
trying to understand the big universe outside, trying to understand why we
are here. The two windows give different views, but both look out at the same
universe. Both views are one-sided, neither is complete. Both leave out
essential features of the real world. And both are worthy of respect.

FREEMAN DYSON

I WOULD LIKE to finish this book by making various connections between science and religion, and showing why I, as a Christian and a scientist, find such wonder in the world, and why, despite the various red flags planted in earlier chapters, I think Christians stand on solid ground.

Christians all have a theology of nature, no matter how vaguely conceived. We believe the world we live in is a *creation*, and we cannot experience it as anything else. That belief illuminates the world for Christian scientists. The belief in the reality of God informs the experience of the wonders of creation.

But our experience of the wonders of creation also informs our understanding of God. If we think of God as rational or loving or artistic or merciful or just or creative, those concepts and definitions take shape in the world we live in, not in some other reality, whatever that might be. If we find the world filled with wonders that move us spiritually or point beyond themselves or inspire us in ways not captured by our explanatory nets, we need not simply shrug our shoulders about why that might be. I think we can reasonably embrace the idea that there must be a transcendent reality in which these experiences are grounded. This, of course, is natural theology, and we must refrain from loud cheering as we draw our conclusions. But there is nothing simple-minded or naively modernist about seeking comprehensive understandings of they way things are, even if we have to "tell less than we can know."

My own thinking about how all this fits together comes from my own internal conversation between my *theology of nature* and my *natural theology*. A Christian theology of nature grows out of our faith tradition. We have ideas about God from a variety of sources—Scripture, our personal experience, the witness of the church. This idea of God provides a framework for understanding the world that God created in its rich complexity. A theology of nature is thus a set of ideas that we

Figure 10.2. This illustration from a 13th century manuscript illustrates the medieval theologians' conviction, based on their natural theology, that God was an architect. Their view of the natural world was dominated by their belief that the earth was at the center of the universe and everything moved about it in perfect circles. (Wikimedia Commons)

bring to the world that shapes how we experience it and respond to it.

Since theology is always open-ended and prepared for revision, any theology of nature must be checked against nature as we encounter it. If, when we take nature on its own terms, it does not meet our expectations, as happened when we discovered that the earth was not at the center of the universe, then we must be prepared to reexamine our theology of nature.

Taking nature on it own terms opens up the natural theology conversation, which we looked at earlier. I am willing to take seriously, if cautiously, these insights. They are rooted in my appreciation for science and the world disclosed by its insights.

Neither God nor nature is a simple reality. Both are sufficiently complex to merit ongoing humble reconsideration.

The rational character of the natural laws that the universe is built on points beyond the physical. This evidence suggests the existence of another reality that we have to take seriously. This is a hint of God. If the universe is grounded in the rationality of God, then it makes sense. If not, the universe is a tale told by an idiot, full of sound and fury (and equations) but signifying nothing.

The fine-tuning of the universe is either an implausible coincidence, a lottery created by the multiverse, or evidence that a Creator designed the universe for life. The third option is the one I choose, and, while qualifications and cautions are in order, I think it is the most reasonable of the options. The Christian tradition informing my values highlights the significance of humans, created in the image of God and given dominion over the earth. I believe that life more or less like that of our species is built into the structure of the universe—that we are intended in some sense to be here, but in a way that does not diminish the value of any other forms of life or give us license to exploit.

The natural trajectory of life toward cooperation and relationship suggests to me that this is more than the simple outworking of some survival equations from game theory. Our deeply rooted affinity for community is a part of the way things are supposed to be. We are intended to love one another. The appreciation that evolutionary biologists now have for the importance of community reveals that they have arrived at insights that Jesus shared with his followers in the first century.

This dialogue between my theology of nature and my natural theology enriches both conversation partners and provides a coherent synthesis that makes the whole more than the sum of the parts. I know more than I can tell. But I am fully convinced that we can know things about the world. We are not mired in local provincial worldviews.

I have never understood the strong form of postmodernity that makes the strange claim that we can know nothing for certain. I once challenged a leading scholar of postmodernity who insisted that all scientific truth was *constructed* by the social activities of the scientific community rather than *discovered,* making every scientific claim relative. "Is the earth round?" I asked her, a professor at one of Boston's leading universities. She hesitated for a rather long time without answering, and said something irrelevant. "Surely we can know the earth is round?" I persisted. "That claim isn't *constructed,* is it?" I said, with growing impatience. "Isn't the claim that the earth is round a *discovery* about the way the world actually *is?*" I pressed her further, but still she would not admit that we can *know* that the earth is round. The conversation ended with me storming off in a most un-Christian manner, muttering to myself that I had just had a conversation with the biggest blockhead in New England.

HUMBLE PIE (BUT NOT TOO HUMBLE)

Postmodernism is among other things a sick joke at the expense of revolutionary avant-gardism.

TERRY EAGLETON

I UNDERSTAND THAT we are living in a postmodern age and have to accept a certain modesty in our claims about the way the world is. Modernity, built on the confidence that one could start with the incontestable facts of the world and build systems of explanation and meaning, has passed. It passed largely because the facts of the world weren't always as incontestable as we had hoped, and because those facts were often so small that they couldn't support anything worthwhile. That was an important lesson. In hindsight we can now see how the prejudices and unexamined assumptions of earlier generations shaped their understanding of the world. Nineteenth-century scientists—all of them male—found ample "evidence" that women pos-

sessed an inferior intelligence. Twentieth-century racists designed IQ
tests that confirmed their prejudices about the relationship between
race and intelligence. We can see that the sexist and racist theories of
yesterday were indeed socially constructed, fabricated from ambiguous
observations stitched together with prejudice and wishful thinking.
We now understand that everyone is embedded in a worldview that
shapes their reflections on the meaning of life and even what they
think are the facts of the world.

Confident assertions that *all* knowledge claims are socially constructed go way too far, however, as my conversation with the postmodern scholar about the shape of the earth makes only too clear. Any
theory of knowledge that can't endorse the claim that the earth is round
should be discarded. In fact, many scientific claims are so well-
established that only an irrational skeptic would have reservations. Can
we seriously doubt that atoms are real, that the earth orbits the sun or
that mammals are warm-blooded? In what sense could the theory of
gravity be a "construction"? Do airplanes fly successfully on a socially
constructed theory of aerodynamics? Sensible people on planes believe
that planes fly because scientists have discovered actual laws of aerodynamics, not made them up.

The obvious truth of so many scientific claims explains why strong
versions of postmodernity are so irrelevant to science. I have never, in
fact, met a postmodern scientist. Not one. Most scientists don't know
what postmodernity is, and when it is explained to them, they are skeptical that anyone could hold such beliefs.

Scientists who think about the nature of knowledge claims—and
this includes me—almost all sign on to an idea known as *critical realism*. We believe there is a real world "out there" to be *discovered* through
careful scientific investigation—not *constructed* from prejudice, duct
tape and fog. We must not claim for our conclusions, however, more
certainty than the evidence warrants. And we must *not* assume that our
conclusions about the world are *absolutely certain*, even though they may
be so probable that such an assumption would create no problems.

All knowledge claims—including those made by science—can be
placed along a spectrum that runs from "merely possible" truths at one

end to "essentially certain" truths at the other. If we number this spectrum from 1 to 100, we would place the belief in life on other planets at 1, since it has no evidence supporting it but is clearly something that could be explored from a scientific perspective. On the other end of the spectrum, perhaps at the point 99.9, we place the belief in the roundness of the earth, since we cannot even imagine how it could be wrong (although we admit that absolute certainty is not warranted, since our knowledge is finite). Other scientific claims lie between these two. I might put the existence of multiple universes at 40, the 5 billion year age for the earth at 95, and the fusion theory of how stars shine at 92. No such scale actually exists in the scientific community, but every scientist will acknowledge that some of their ideas are more certain than others.

GRASPING AFTER TRUTH

The pursuit of truth will set you free,
even if you never catch up with it.

CLARENCE DARROW

The truth will set you free.

JESUS OF NAZARETH

CRITICAL REALISTS BELIEVE that the world is known through a spiraling discovery process where we continually circle the phenomena we are trying to understand, getting closer and closer as we understand it better, but never reaching absolute certainty. A gap always exists between the thing we want to understand and our very best theory of how that thing works. The gap can be small or large, but it never entirely vanishes.

We can also use critical realism in our theology. We can accept, as a starting point, the existence of a transcendent reality—God—that exists "out there." The starting point for this belief can be based on our faith tradition, our personal experience or even the arguments of the natural theologians. It doesn't matter where we get our ideas—Dirac got some of his ideas from beauty—as long as we are prepared to test those ideas against our experience of the world. We acknowledge—in theology, as in science—that we can understand this reality only through dialogue, as we constantly test and refine our understanding, spiraling in on the truth. Theological results will never have the grand simplicity of the theory of gravity, but that is because gravity is simple and God is complicated, not because gravity exists and God does not.

As a critical realist who takes both science and theology—and a lot of other things—seriously, I am drawn to make connections between all the various things I think are true. I am mindful of the cautions discussed earlier, of course. But there is a big difference between the claim that, say, the fine-tuning of the universe proves the existence of God, and the more modest claim that fine-tuning fits comfortably, supportively and logically within a worldview grounded in the belief that God is the Creator of all that is. This is both an easier claim to make and a much more profound claim.

The same is true for all the hints of God. As traditional natural theology arguments, the various scientific pointers, from the beauty of sunsets to the mysterious carbon resonance, are just hints (see inserts Figures R-S). They don't take us very far. But as components in a larger worldview, they provide valuable confirmation, just as Eddington's measurement of a tiny shift in the position of a star provided a valuable confirmation of a far-reaching and comprehensive theory of how the universe works.

The Christian worldview, with its belief in a God who creates and is revealed in the exemplary life, death and resurrection of Jesus, is the starting point from which we examine the mystery of our existence— *the wonder of the universe*. We live in a world of immense beauty, from sunsets to equations, from music to children's laughter. We live in a world of great meaning and find ourselves bound to each other by love—a love that seems as deeply embedded in reality as atoms and molecules. But we also live in a world of great suffering. Wars, natural disasters, sickness and death all conspire to drain the meaning from life and replace it with despair. Human selfishness and frivolous indulgence tempt us toward apathy. But the Christian worldview demands that we view those features of our world as alien interlopers, superficial anomalies to be dispatched and dissolved. The beauty and wonder of the world is the real part.

As we come to understand this world, we discover the deep and profound *adequacy* of the Christian worldview as it illuminates so much of what we experience, informs so much of what we do and calls us to the highest standards of service to our fellow human beings and the creation in general.

> If I have been enticed into brashness
> by the wonderful beauty of thy works,
> or if I have loved my own glory among men,
> while advancing in work destined for thy glory,
> gently and mercifully pardon me:
> and finally,
> deign graciously to cause that these demonstrations
> may lead to thy glory and to the salvation of souls,
> and nowhere be an obstacle to that.
> Amen.

—Johannes Kepler, *The Harmony of the World* (1619)

ACKNOWLEDGMENTS

The Wonder of the Universe: Hints of God in a Fine-Tuned World was originally proposed by Andy LePeau, my editor at InterVarsity Press, as a sequel to my earlier book with Francis Collins, *The Language of Science and Faith: Straight Answers to Genuine Questions.* The goal was a faith-friendly "science and religion" book that would fly above the ubiquitous fog of the creation-evolution controversy. I want to thank Andy for getting the ball rolling and then keeping it on track as it careened from vision to reality.

We decided early on that the book would benefit from the inclusion of images, which adds greatly to the complexity of the project at several levels. I would like to thank Brooke Sword and Carissa Schutz, two of my former students at Eastern Nazarene College, for their efforts at helping secure the permissions needed to include so many images in this book. And I especially thank Elaina Whittenhall at InterVarsity Press for her tireless efforts on behalf of images. The process occasionally made me a bit cranky, and I thank everyone for putting up with me.

Two readers made very helpful suggestions on the first draft. An anonymous astronomy professor read and fact-checked the entire draft, finding factual errors and other things that needed attention. That input was critically important and deeply appreciated. And the ever-present Andy LePeau identified several places that needed work, including a final chapter that needed to be totally rewritten. He confirms one of the basic truths of writing that I have learned over the years: *a writer has no better friend than a good editor.*

My student assistant Katie Brinegar read the entire manuscript in page proofs and helped prepare the index. She also caught a few editorial problems that had escaped the eyes of more experienced readers.

For most of the writing of *The Wonder of the Universe* I was supported by the BioLogos Foundation, founded by Francis Collins, and underwritten by grants from the Templeton Foundation and other sources.

Being supported to write is an author's fantasy, of course, and I am grateful to Francis for inviting me to get involved with BioLogos. (Readers interested in evangelical perspectives on the intersection of science and faith will find helpful material at www.biologos.org.)

And lastly, I would like to thank my loving wife, Myrna, who has supported me and my irregular writing career for more years than I care to remember. It is to her that this book is affectionately dedicated.

Karl Giberson

BIBLIOGRAPHY

A WIDE-RANGING BOOK LIKE THIS draws heavily on a lifetime of reading, and I cannot recall all the books that have shaped my thinking on these various topics. Nor do I even want to remember all the books that I have read, and there are many I cannot recommend. As I have gotten older and invested increasingly more time in the craft of writing, I have grown impatient with authors whose interest in writing seems to extend no further than getting their ideas on paper, with no concern for the experience of their readers as they try to get those ideas off of that paper and into their heads.

With that prejudice as a sieve eliminating most of the books in the Library of Congress on this topic, I offer the following as a guide to further reading. You can rest assured that every book recommended in this brief discussion, with a few exceptions, has been written with care and attention for the quality of the reading experience. Inadvertent omissions from this list simply mean the book was not on my bookcases or in my Kindle.

The remarkable story of long-time philosopher Antony Flew's transformation from atheist to theist is told in *There Is a God: How the World's Most Notorious Atheist Changed His Mind* by Antony Flew, with Roy Abraham Varghese. The book is lively and written in first person. There is some interesting speculation that Flew's coauthor Varghese manipulated both Flew and the subsequent "testimony." The best account of this is Mark Oppenheimer's "The Turning of an Atheist," which can be found at www.nytimes.com/2007/11/04/magazine/04 Flew-t.html?_r=1.

David Park's *The Grand Contraption: The World as Myth, Number, and Chance* presents many of the ancient worldviews with an engaging sympathy. Appreciating just how different these ancient worldviews were is critically important, especially for those of us tempted to read modern science into the biblical creation stories.

The history of astronomy and cosmology has attracted many great writers over the years. The best-written, hands down, is Timothy Ferris's *Coming of Age in the Milky Way*. Ferris's lively and informed writing has long been an inspiration to me. I also recommend the sequel, *The Whole Shebang: A State-of-the-Universe(s) Report*. Two other helpful volumes by Dartmouth College astronomer Marcelo Gleiser are *The Dancing Universe: From Creation Myths to the Big Bang* and *The Prophet and the Astronomer: A Scientific Journey to the End of Time*. The former commits the common historical error of accusing first-millennium Christians of being flat-earthers. (*Coming of Age* by Ferris does the same thing, which led to my repeating the same uninformed slander in my first book *Worlds Apart: The Unholy War Between Religion and Science*.) Although dated and idiosyncratic, I still love *The Sleepwalkers: A History of Man's Changing Vision of the Universe* by Arthur Koestler, one of the great writers of the twentieth century. His history of astronomy from ancient Greece through Newton, first published in 1959 and still in print, is as close to a page turner on this subject as one can get. *The View from the Center of the Universe: Discovering Our Extraordinary Place in the Cosmos* by physicist Joel Primack and the award-winning writer Nancy Ellen Abrams is an excellent secular reflection on many of the same themes as this book.

There are wonderful biographies of the key players in the history of astronomy, all of which make great reading. Readers wanting to look at the scientific revolution as it unfolded can start with *Copernicus' Secret: How the Scientific Revolution Began* by Jack Repcheck, and Owen Gingerich's *The Book Nobody Read: Chasing the Revolutions of Nicolaus Copernicus*. *On Tycho's Island: Tycho Brahe, Science & Culture in the Sixteenth Century* by John Robert Christianson is a recent biography of the greatest astronomer of the pretelescopic era. James A. Connors's captivating *Kepler's Witch: An Astronomer's Discovery of Cosmic Order Amid Religious War, Political Intrigue, and the Heresy Trial of His Mother* deserves to be made into a Hollywood movie; Dava Sobel's, *Galileo's Daughter: A His-*

torical Memoir of Science, Faith, and Love is a beautifully written story of Galileo, enriched by discussion of his deep and abiding love for his daughter. Sobel is one of the best nonfiction writers working in the English language. *Newton's Gift: How Sir Isaac Newton Unlocked the System of the World* by David Berlinski is a brief biography of the great scientist. I wrote a lengthy account of Newton's achievement titled "The Warden of Time and Space" for *Books & Culture*.[1] The ambitious and definitive *Einstein: His Life and Universe* by Walter Isaacson is a recent *New York Times* bestseller. Matthew Stanley's *Practical Mystic: Religion, Science, and A. S. Eddington* is a wide-ranging and well-informed look at the implications of the new cosmology that emerged in the early twentieth century. *The Day Without Yesterday: Lemaître, Einstein, and the Birth of Modern Cosmology* by John Farrel provides useful insights into the life of Bishop Lemaître, one of the more obscure figures in twentieth-century cosmology.

Readers interested in knowing more about the planets need look no further than Sobel's small volume *The Planets*.

Chemistry is the most important of the sciences, in terms of its relevance to humans, but also the most difficult to make interesting. Engaging books on astronomy probably outnumber those on chemistry by ten to one. *Napoleon's Buttons: How 17 Molecules Changed History* by Penny Le Couteur and Jay Burreson does a great job of showing just how entwined our lives are with atoms and molecules. Nobel Laureate Christian de Duve's *Vital Dust: Life as a Cosmic Imperative* argues that life emerges smoothly and naturally when the conditions are right. Paul Davies, cosmologist and this generation's most influential popularizer of physics, counters de Duve in *The Fifth Miracle: The Search for the Origin and Meaning of Life*. Davies argues that known processes cannot account for the origin of life and that we need new scientific ideas if we want to understand life. Readers would also do well to ponder the provocative thesis of *Rare Earth: Why Complex Life Is Uncommon in the Universe* by Peter D. Ward and Donald Brownlee, which argues that the conditions needed for life are so incredibly specific that we should not suppose that life is common in the universe.

Many books discuss the fine-tuning of the universe from a variety of perspectives. *God's Universe* by Owen Gingerich is a delightful small book containing the text of Gingerich's Noble lectures. Gingerich is a longtime member of the faculty at Harvard University, a committed Christian believer and a close personal friend. *Cosmic Jackpot: Why Our Universe Is Just Right for Life* by Paul Davies provides a balanced treatment of the topic. Davies is a skeptic who is sympathetic and informed on questions of theology. The standard scholarly work on this topic is the magisterial *The Anthropic Cosmological Principle* by John Barrow and Frank Tipler. With over 1,500 endnotes and countless equations, it is not for the faint of heart, and I recommend it only to readers with doctoral degrees in physics or astronomy. Martin Rees's small classic *Just Six Numbers: The Deep Forces That Shape the Universe* does a good job of showing how a few brute facts shape the universe, without inferring any design. The atheistic and antireligious physicist Vic Stenger has written several books critiquing belief in God, especially those based on design arguments. *The Fallacy of Fine Tuning: Why the Universe Is Not Designed for Us* is his most recent and offers an informed counter to the very argument that led Antony Flew to belief in God.

The field of science and religion has exploded in recent years, largely because of generous support from the Templeton Foundation, which, via the BioLogos Foundation, also supported me in the writing of this book. I recommend the following five anthologies, all of which dig deeper into the subject material of this book:

- *When Science and Christianity Meet* edited by David C. Lindberg and Ronald L. Numbers

- *God and Nature: Historical Essays on the Encounter Between Christianity and Science* edited by David C. Linberg and Ronald L. Numbers

- *Science and Religion: A Historical Introduction* edited by Gary B. Ferngren

- *Reappraisals of the Scientific Revolution* edited by David C. Lindberg and Robert S. Westman

- *Evangelicals and Science in Historical Perspective* edited by David Livingstone, D. G. Hart and Mark A. Noll

Readers interested in the philosophy of science should read *What Science Knows and How It Knows It* by James Franklin, which I reviewed positively for the *Weekly Standard*. I also recommend Derek Gjertsen's *Science and Philosophy: Past and Present*, which looks at how the boundaries defining science have changed constantly through time.

The previous books are all essentially "secular" in the sense that they are not written from an explicitly Christian perspective. Even the books by Flew and Gingerich, which support belief in God, have no explicitly Christian component. Flew, in fact, rejects Christianity. But many well-informed scholars have taken up the task of integrating science with traditional Christian theology and biblical interpretation.

Alister McGrath is the leading and most prolific evangelical theologian who considers issues related to science and religion. His 2009 Gifford Lectures, *Fine-Tuned Universe: The Quest for God in Science and Theology*, provides an updated review of natural theology—treated more as a theology of nature—by one of Christianity's best informed theologians. Also of value is McGrath's three-volume set *A Scientific Theology*, subtitled (1) *Nature*, (2) *Reality* and (3) *Theory*. This ambitious project covers all the bases.

In Defense of Natural Theology: A Post-Humean Assessment edited by James F. Sennett and Douglas Groothuis defends traditional natural theology.

I recommend three books on approaches to the Bible, all written by current or former scholars at evangelical colleges: *Science, Creation, and the Bible: Reconciling Rival Theories of Origins* by Richard F. Carlson and Tremper Longman III; *The Lost World of Genesis One: Ancient Cosmology and the Origins Debate* by John H. Walton; *Inspiration and Incarnation: Evangelicals and the Problem of the Old Testament* by Peter Enns. All of them suggest approaches to Genesis that greatly reduce the tension between the Bible and scientific theories of origins.

Davis Young's *The Biblical Flood: A Case Study of the Church's Response to Extrabiblical Evidence* offers a helpful historical survey that illuminates the questions discussed in this book and shows that Christianity has the capacity to adapt to scientific advances.

Ian Barbour's *When Science Meets Religion: Enemies, Strangers, or*

Partners? is a great way to get started thinking about the integration of science and Christian theology.

For readers concerned about the interaction of biological evolution and Christian theology I recommend any of the books on the topic by two Catholic authors: biologist Ken Miller of Brown University and theologian John Haught of Georgetown. Francis Collins's bestseller, *The Language of God: A Scientist Presents Evidence for Belief*, is probably the single most helpful book by an evangelical on evolution.

Finally, if you like the approach I have taken in this book and would like to explore my other books, here they are:

- *Worlds Apart: The Unholy War Between Religion and Science*

- *Species of Origins: America's Search for a Creation Story*

- *Oracles of Science: Celebrity Scientists Versus God and Religion* (with Mariano Artigas)

- *Saving Darwin: How to be a Christian and Believe in Evolution*

- *The Language of Science and Faith: Straight Answers to Genuine Questions* (with Francis Collins)

- *Quantum Leap: How John Polkinghorne Found God in Science and Religion* (with Dean Nelson)

- *The Anointed: Evangelical Truth in a Secular Age* (with Randall Stephens)

- *And God Saw That It Was Good: A Creation Story for the 21st Century* (forthcoming, 2012)

NOTES

Introduction: Following the Evidence Where It Leads

[1] Antony Flew, with Roy Abraham Varghese, *There Is a God: How the World's Most Notorious Atheist Changed His Mind* (New York: HarperOne, 2007), p. 10.

[2] "Welcome to Kingswood," *Kingswood*, accessed June 2, 2011, www.kingswood .bath.sch.uk/index.php.

[3] Flew, *There Is a God*, pp. 10-11.

[4] Antony Flew, "My Pilgrimage from Atheism to Theism: An Exclusive Interview with Former British Atheist Professor Antony Flew," by Gary Habermas, *Philosophia Christi*, winter 2005.

[5] Mark Oppenheimer, "The Turning of an Atheist," *New York Times*, November 4, 2007, www.nytimes.com/2007/11/04/magazine/04Flew-t.html.

[6] Immanuel Kant, *Critique of Practical Reason* (Mineola, NY: Dover Publications, 2004), p. 170.

[7] Raphael G. Satter, "Farthest-Ever Explosion Found at Edge of Cosmos?" *Guardian*, May 29, 2011, www.guardian.co.uk/world/feedarticle/9670137.

Chapter 1: Learning to Read the Book of Nature

[1] Pratyush Tiwari, "The Fall of Icarus," *Boloji.com*, January 6, 2002, www.boloji.com/ poetry/1401-1500/1439.htm.

[2] Andrew Dickson White, *A History of the Warfare of Science with Theology in Christendom* (New York: Free Press, 1965), p. 247.

[3] Nicolaus Copernicus, quoted in Dava Sobel, *Galileo's Daughter: A Historical Memoir of Science, Faith, and Love* (New York: Walker, 1999), p. 50.

[4] Sobel, *Galileo's Daughter*, p. 6.

[5] Johannes Kepler, quoted in *The Complete Book of Christian Prayer* (New York: Continuum, 1995), p. 26.

[6] Isaac Newton, *Sir Isaac Newton's Mathematical Principles of Natural Philosophy and His System of the World*, ed. Florian Cajori, trans. Andrew Motte (Berkeley: University of California Press, 1962), 2:543-47.

[7] "Collected Quotes of Albert Einstein," accessed August 24, 2011, http://rescomp .stanford.edu/~cheshire/EinsteinQuotes.html.

[8] Galileo Galilei, *The Assayer*, in *The Controversy of the Comets of 1618*, ed. Stillman Drake (Philadelphia: University of Pennsylvania Press, 1960), p. 232.

Chapter 2: A Wonderful World

[1]"Mercury Facts and Figures," NASA, accessed June 2, 2011, http://solarsystem.nasa.gov/planets/profile.cfm?Object=Mercury&Display=Facts&System=Metric.

[2]Fraser Cain, "Orbit of Pluto," UniverseToday.com, April 24, 2008, www.universeto day.com/13865/orbit-of-pluto.

[3]"The Solar System: The Oort Cloud," *Interactive Library*, accessed June 2, 2011, www.edinformatics.com/math_science/solar_system/oort_cloud.htm.

[4]Fraser Cain, "How Many Miles Around the Earth," UniverseToday.com, June 16, 2010, www.universetoday.com/66515/how-many-miles-around-the-earth.

[5]Fraser Cain, "Distance from Earth to Moon," UniverseToday.com, August 23, 2009, www.universetoday.com/38128/distance-from-earth-to-moon.

[6]Ian O'Neill, "How Long Does it Take to Get to the Moon?" UniverseToday.com, April 10, 2008, www.universetoday.com/13562/how-long-does-it-take-to-get-to-the-moon.

[7]Fraser Cain, "Distance from Earth to Mars," UniverseToday.com, June 4, 2008, www.universetoday.com/14824/distance-from-earth-to-mars.

[8]Diane Fisher, "Packing for a L-o-o-o-ng Trip to Mars," *The Technology Teacher*, December 2001, accessed from NASA website on August 9, 2011, http://shuttle experience.nasa.gov/KidsCorner/PackMars.pdf.

[9]Fraser Cain, "Distance to Pluto," UniverseToday.com, April 26, 2008, www.uni versetoday.com/13891/distance-to-pluto.

[10]"The Solar System: The Oort Cloud."

[11]Ibid.

[12]Carl Sagan, Pale Blue Dot: A Vision of the Human Future in Space (New York: Random House, 1994), p. 7.

[13]"How Big Is Our Universe?" NASA, accessed June 2, 2011, www.nasa.gov/audi ence/foreducators/5-8/features/F_How_Big_is_Our_Universe.html. These distances are so great they cannot really be visualized. There are websites that help with this. See, for example, http://heasarc.nasa.gov/docs/cosmic/milkyway_info.html.

Chapter 3: Learning to See the Universe

[1]Michael Fowler, "Galileo and the Telescope," Galileo and Einstein, accessed September 12, 2010, http://galileoandeinstein.physics.virginia.edu/lectures/galtel.htm.

[2]Galileo, quoted in Timothy Ferris, *Coming of Age in the Milky Way* (New York: HarperCollins, 2003), p. 88.

[3]Ibid.

[4]Fred Watson, *Stargazer: The Life and Times of the Telescope* (Cambridge, Mass.: De Capo, 2004), p. 79.

[5]Deborah Houlding, "The Irrepressible Galileo Galilei," *Traditional Astrologer* 15 (October 1997): 18-23.

[6]Isaac Newton, quoted in Timothy Ferris, *Coming of Age in the Milky Way* (New York: HarperCollins, 2003), p. 105.

[7]Stephen Hawking and Werner Israel, "The Answer Is No," *The Times*, London, 27 June 1987.

[8]"Discovery of Neptune," *Wikipedia*, accessed June 7, 2011, http://en.wikipedia.org/wiki/Discovery_of_Neptune.

[9]Albert Einstein, quoted in "Albert Einstein: Impact and Image," American Institute of Physics, www.aip.org/history/einstein/ae17.htm.

Chapter 4: The Wonder of the Cosmos

[1]John Hedley Brooke, *Science and Religion: Some Historical Perspectives* (Cambridge: Cambridge University Press, 1991), pp. 189-90.

[2]Karl Giberson, "The Patent Clerk from Mount Olympus," *Books & Culture*, November-December 2005.

[3]Albert Einstein, quoted in Kip S. Thorne, *Black Holes and Time Warps: Einstein's Outrageous Legacy* (New York: W. W. Norton, 1995), p. 160.

[4]Michael Polanyi, *Personal Knowledge* (Chicago: University of Chicago Press, 1958), pp. 266-67.

[5]John Farrel, *The Day Without Yesterday: LeMaitre, Einstein, and the Birth of Modern Cosmology* (New York: Thunder's Mouth, 2005), p. 27.

[6]Arthur Eddington, quoted in Farrel, *Day Without Yesterday*, p. 106.

[7]Ibid., p. 108.

[8]Helge Kragh, "Steady State Theory," *Cosmology: Historical, Literary, Philosophical, Religious, and Scientific Perspectives*, ed. Norriss S. Hetherington (New York: Garland, 1993), p. 393.

[9]Technically, the categories are quarks and leptons, but the electron is the most important and familiar lepton, so I am going to ignore the many other, lesser leptons.

Chapter 5: Living on a Goldilocks Planet

[1]Seth Borenstein, "Could 'Goldilocks' Planet Be Just Right for Life?" *Guardian News and Media*, September 30, 2010, accessed June 7, 2011, www.guardian.co.uk/world/feedarticle/9288661.

[2]David Derbyshire, "I'd Love to Baptize ET, Says Vatican's Stargazer," September 17, 2010, accessed June 7, 2011, www.dailymail.co.uk/sciencetech/article-1312922/Pope-astronomer-Guy-Consolmagno-Aliens-souls-living-stars.html.

[3]Ken Ham, "I'd Love to Baptise an Alien," *Around the World with Ken Ham, Answers Outreach*, September 23, 2010, http://blogs.answersingenesis.org/blogs/ken-ham/2010/09/23/%E2%80%9Ci%E2%80%99d-love-to-baptise-an-alien%E2%80%9D.

[4]Bruce Dorminey, "Dark Forces," *Cosmos* 16 (August 2007), www.cosmosmagazine.com/node/2704/full.

Chapter 6: Monkeying with the Physics

[1]Technically, the term *contact* is not appropriate here, since protons don't have surfaces like marbles. But no confusion—and much illumination—results from using this simplified picture.

[2]Paul Davies, *Cosmic Jackpot: Why Our Universe Is Just Right for Life* (New York: Houghton-Mifflin, 2007), p. 146.

[3]Freeman Dyson, *Disturbing the Universe* (New York: Basic Books, 2001), p. 250.

Interlude: Crossing the Uncertain Bridge

[1]"The Arsenic Paper Is Out, Along with Eight Critiques," *Why Evolution Is True,* accessed June 5, 2011, http://whyevolutionistrue.wordpress.com/2011/06/05/the-arsenic-paper-is-out-along-with-eight-critiques.

[2]"Francis Bacon," *Wikipedia*, accessed June 17, 2011, http://en.wikipedia.org/wiki/Francis_Bacon.

[3]"Astronomers Find First Evidence of Other Universes," *Technology Review*, December 13, 2010, www.technologyreview.com/blog/arxiv/26132/?ref=rss; and John Horgan, "Is Speculation in Multiverses as Immoral as Speculation in Subprime Mortgages?" *Scientific American*, January 28, 2011, www.scientificamerican.com/blog/post.cfm?id=is-speculation-in-multiverses-as-im-2011-01-28.

Chapter 7: Is This the "Best of All Possible Worlds"?

[1]Voltaire, *Candide* (Sioux Falls, S.D.: NuVision, 2007), p. 8.

[2]Christopher Hitchens, quoted in Mariano Grinbank, "Christopher Hitchens—The Atheopic Principle," True Freethinker, accessed June 14, 2011, www.truefree thinker.com/articles/christopher-hitchens-atheopic-principle.

[3]Hugh Ross, "Astronomical Evidences for a Personal, Transcendent God," *The Creation Hypothesis*, ed. J. P. Moreland (Downers Grove, Ill.: InterVarsity Press, 1994), p. 164.

[4]William Paley, *Natural Theology* (New York: Oxford University Press, 2006), p. 7.

Chapter 8: Following the Evidence

[1]Stephen Jay Gould, *Wonderful Life: The Burgess Shale and the Nature of History* (New York: W. W. Norton, 1989), quoted in Richard E. Lenski, "The Eyes Have It," *Nature* 425, no. 6960 (2003), p. 767.

[2]Gould, *Wonderful Life,* p. 289.

[3]Ibid., pp. 141-45.

[4]Simon Conway Morris, "We Were Meant to Be . . . ," *New Scientist* 176, no. 2369 (2002): 26.

[5]Simon Conway Morris, *Life's Solution: Inevitable Humans in a Lonely Universe* (New York: Cambridge University Press, 2003).

[6]Morris, "We Were Meant to Be . . . ," p. 26.

[7]Morris, *Life's Solution.*

[8]Karl Giberson and Francis Collins. *The Language of Faith and Science: Straight Answers to Genuine Questions* (Downers Grove, Ill.: InterVarsity Press, 2011), pp. 204-5.

[9]Robert Wright, "Introduction," *Nonzero: The Logic of Human Destiny*, accessed June 14, 2011, www.nonzero.org/intro.htm.

[10]Robert Wright, *The Evolution of God* (New York: Little, Brown, 2009), p. 458.

[11]Robert Wright, quoted in Steve Paulson, "God, He's Moody," Salon.com, June 24, 2009, www.salon.com/news/environment/atoms_eden/2009/06/24/evolution_of_god.

[12]Ibid.

Chapter 9: Cautious Optimism

[1]Richard Dawkins, "Why There Almost Certainly Is No God," www.against religions.org/en/blog/post_15/, accessed August 9, 2011.

[2]Stephen Hawking, *A Brief History of Time: From the Big Bang to Black Holes* (Toronto: Bantam Books, 1988), p. 155.

[3]Brian Greene, The Hidden Reality: Parallel Universes and the Deep Laws of the Cosmos (New York: Alfred A. Knopf, 2011).

[4]Stephen Hawking and Leonard Miodinow, *The Grand Design* (New York: Bantam Books, 2010), cited in Karl Giberson, "Hawking's Speculation: Everything Happens," The Huffington Post, September 9, 2010, www.huffingtonpost.com/karl-giberson-phd/hawkings-speculation-ever_b_703374.html.

[5]Max Tegmark, "Parallel Universes," *Scientific American*, May 2003, http://space.mit.edu/home/tegmark/PDF/multiverse_sciam.pdf.

[6] Stephen Hawking and Leonard Mlodinow, *The Grand Design* (New York: Bantam Books, 2010), p. 180.

[7]Paul Davies, *Cosmic Jackpot: Why Our Universe Is Just Right for Life* (New York: Houghton Mifflin, 2007), p. 173.

[8]Ibid.

Chapter 10: It's a Wonderful World

[1]Jerry A. Coyne, *Why Evolution Is True*, July 7, 2011, http://whyevolutionistrue.word press.com/2011/07/07/john-horgan-responds-defends-wishful-thinking/.

[2]Albert Einstein, http://rescomp.stanford.edu/~cheshire/EinsteinQuotes.html; Paul Dirac, www-history.mcs.st-and.ac.uk/Quotations/Dirac.html; and Eugene Wigner, www.dartmouth.edu/~matc/MathDrama/reading/Wigner.html.

[3]Freeman Dyson, *Disturbing the Universe* (New York: Basic Books, 2001), p. 250.

Bibliography

[1] This can be found at www.karlgiberson.com/writing.

Index